# CCNA Cisco Certified Network Associate

## COMPILED BY

## OLUWASEGUN AINA

# Q &A

**1. Which statements about using leased lines for your WAN infrastructure are true? (choose 2 options)**

A. cdp enable

B. cdp run

C. enable cdp

D. run cdp

**2. Which condition does the err-disabled status indicate on an Ethernet interface? choose 1 options**

A. The device at the other end of the connection is powered off.

B. There is a duplex mismatch.

C. Port security has disabled Step 1:Click on the console host, you will get a pop-up screen CLI of Router. Router> the interface.

D. The serial interface is disabled.

E. The interface is fully functioning.

**3. Which condition indicates that service password-encryption is enabled? choose 1 options**

A. The local username password is encrypted in the configuration.

B. The enable secret is in clear text in the configuration.

C. The local username password is in clear text in the configuration.

D. The enable secret is encrypted in the configuration.

4. Which type of device can be replaced by the use of sub-interfaces for VLAN routing? choose 1 options

A. Layer 2 bridge

B. router

C. Layer 3 switch

D. Layer 2 switch

5. Which command can you enter to determine whether serial interface 0/2/0 has been configured using HDLC encapsulation? choose 1 options

A. router#show interfaces Serial 0/2/0

B. router#show platform

C. router#show ip interface brief

D. router#show ip interface s0/2/0

6. Which Layer 2 protocol encapsulation type supports synchronous and asynchronous circuits and has built-in security mechanisms? choose 1 options

A. HDLC

B. Frame Relay

C. PPP

D. X.25

7. Refer to the exhibit

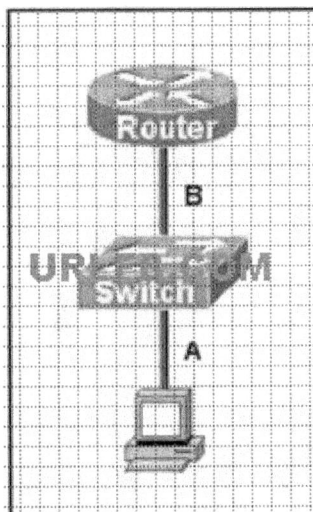

The two connected ports on the switch are not turning orange or green
Which three would be the most effective steps to troubleshoot this physical layer problem? (Choose three)

A. Ensure cable A is plugged into a trunk port

B. Ensure the switch has power

C. Ensure that the Ethernet encapsulations match on the interconnected router and switch ports

D. Ensure that cables A and B are straight-through cables.

E. Reboot all of the devices

8. Which statements about IPv6 prefixes are true? choose 3 options

A. FC00::/7 is used in private networks.

B. FEC0::/10 is used for IPv6 broadcast.

C. FE80::/10 is used for link-local unicast

D. FE80::/8 is used for link-local unicast.

E. FF00::/8 is used for IPv6 multicast.

9. Which command can you enter to display duplicate IP addresses that the DHCP server assigns? choose 1 options

A. show ip dhcp server statistics

B. show ip dhcp database 10.0.2.12

C. show ip dhcp binding 10.0.2.12

D. show ip dhcp conflict 10.0.2.12

10. What are advantages of VLANs? choose 3 options

A. They can simplify adding, moving, or changing hosts on the network.
B. They establish broadcast domains in switched networks.
C. They allow access to network services based on department, not physical location.
D. They provide a low-latency internetworking alternative to routed networks.
E. They utilize packet filtering to enhance network security.

11. Scenario. Refer to the topology
Your company has decided to connect the main office with three Other remote branch offices using point-to-point serial links.
You are required to troubleshoot and resolve OSPF neighbor adjacency issues

between the main office and the routers located in the remote branch offices_
Use appropriate show commands to troubleshoot the issues and answer all four questions
Instructions

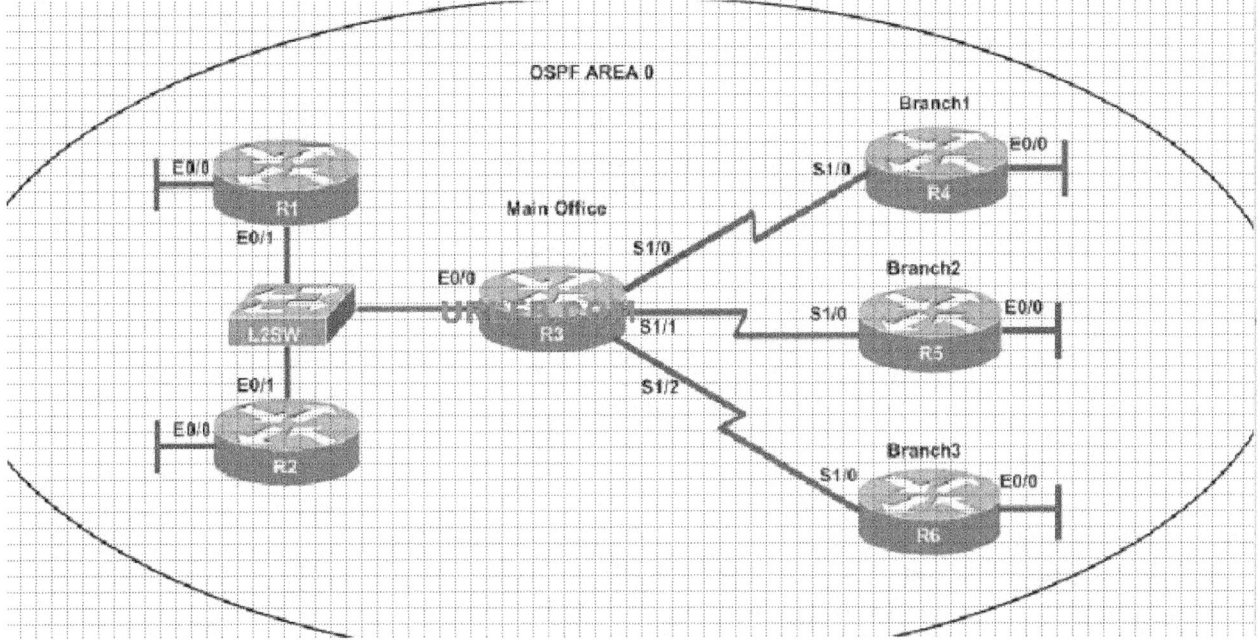

An OSPF neighbor adjacency is not formed between R3 in the main office and R4 in the Branch1 office. What is causing the problem?

A. There is an area ID mismatch

B. There is a Layer 2 issue; an encapsulation mismatch on serial links.

C. The R3 router ID is configured on R4

D. There is an OSPF hello and dead interval mismatch

12. Your company has decided to connect the main office with three Other remote branch offices using point-to-point serial links. You are required to troubleshoot and resolve OSPF neighbor adjacency issues between the main office and the routers located in the remote branch offices_Use appropriate show commands to troubleshoot the issues and answer all four questions Instructions

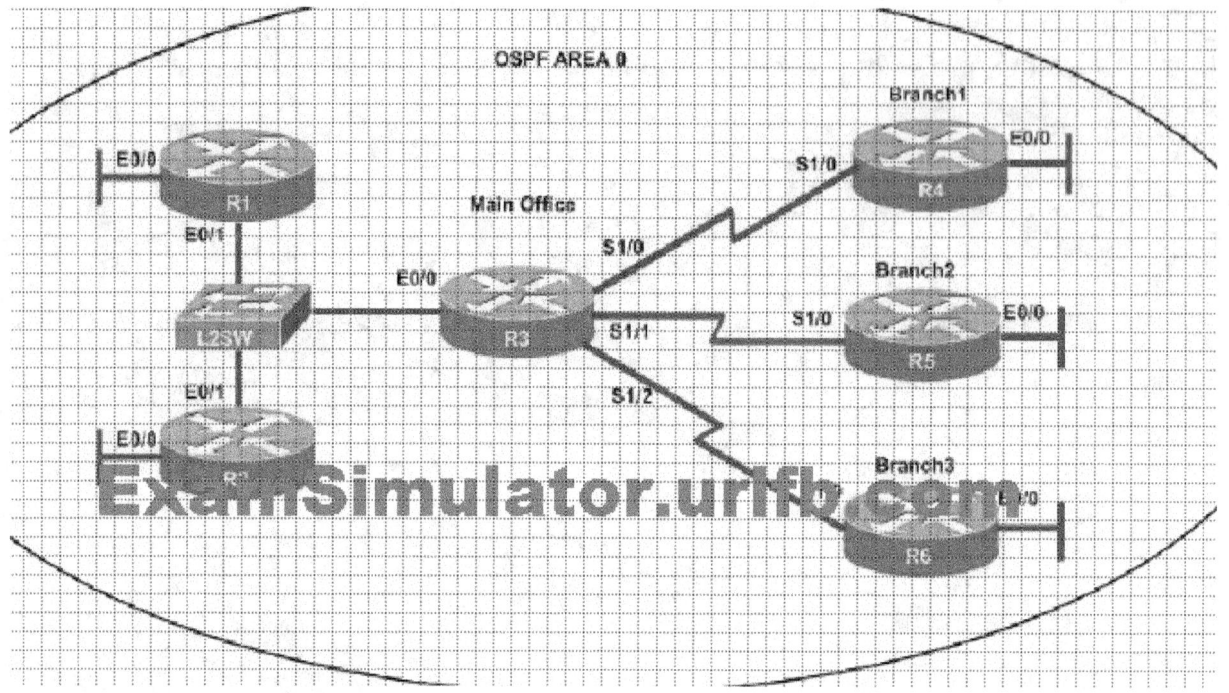

An OSPF neighbor adjacency is not formed between R3 in the main office and R5 in the Branch2 office. What is causing the problem?

A. There is an area ID mismatch

B. There is a PPP authentication issue; a password mismatch

C. There is an OSPF hello and dead interval mismatch

D. There is a missing network command in the OSPF process on R5

13. During which phase of PPPoE is PPP authentication performed? choose 1 options

A. Phase 2

B. the PPP Session phase

C. Phase 1

D. the Authentication phase

E. the Active Discovery phase

14. What is the authoritative source for an address lookup? choose 1 options

A. the operating system cache

B. a recursive DNS search

C. the browser cache

D. the ISP local cache

**15. An engineer is troubleshooting an EIGRP problem on a router and needs to confirm the IP addresses of the devices with which the router has established adjacency. The retransmit interval and the queue counts for the adjacent routers also need to be checked. What command will display the required information?choose 1 options**

A. show ip eigrp neighbors

**16. Which function of the IP SLAs ICMP jitter operation can you use to determine whether a VoIP issue is caused by excessive end-to-end time?choose 1 options**

A. packet loss

B. round-trip time latency

C. jitter

D. successive packet loss

**17. Which statements about IPv4 multicast traffic are true?choose 2 options**

A. It simultaneously delivers multiple streams of data.

B. It burdens the source host without affecting remote hosts.

C. It uses a minimum amount of network bandwidth.

D. It is the most efficient way to deliver data to multiple receivers.

E. It is bandwidth-intensive.

**18. What are characteristics of the TCP protocol?choose 3 options**

A. The connection is established before data is transmitted.

B. It ensures that all data is transmitted and received by the remote device

C. It uses a single SYN-ACK message to establish a connection.

D. It supports significantly higher transmission speeds than UDP.

E. It uses separate SYN and ACK messages to establish a connection.

**19. What are reasons that duplex mismatches can be difficult to diagnose? choose 2 options**

A. 1-Gbps interfaces are full-duplex by default.

B. Full-duplex interfaces use CSMA/CD logic, so mismatches may be disguised by collisions.

C. The symptoms of a duplex mismatch may be intermittent.

D. The interface displays a connected (up/up) state even when the duplex settings are mismatched.

E. Autonegotiation is disabled.

**20. Which command can you enter to verify that a 128-bit address is live and responding? Choose 1 options**

A. telnet

B. traceroute

C. ping ipv6

D. ping

**21. When an interface is configured with PortFast BPDU guard, how does the interface respond when it receives a BPDU? choose 1 options**

A. It becomes the root bridge for the configured VLAN.

B. It goes into a down/down state.

C. It goes into an errdisable state.

D. It continues operating normally.

**22. Which statement about RADIUS security is true? Choose 1 options**

A. It ensures that user activity is fully anonymous.

B. It supports EAP authentication for connecting to wireless networks.

C. It provides encrypted multiprotocol support.

D. Device-administration packets are encrypted in their entirety.

**23. Scenario**
**Refer to the topology**
**Your company has decided to connect the main office with three Other remote branch offices using point-to-point serial links.**
**You are required to troubleshoot and resolve OSPF neighbor adjacency issues between the main office and the routers located in the remote branch offices**

Use appropriate show commands to troubleshoot the issues and answer all four questions

Instructions

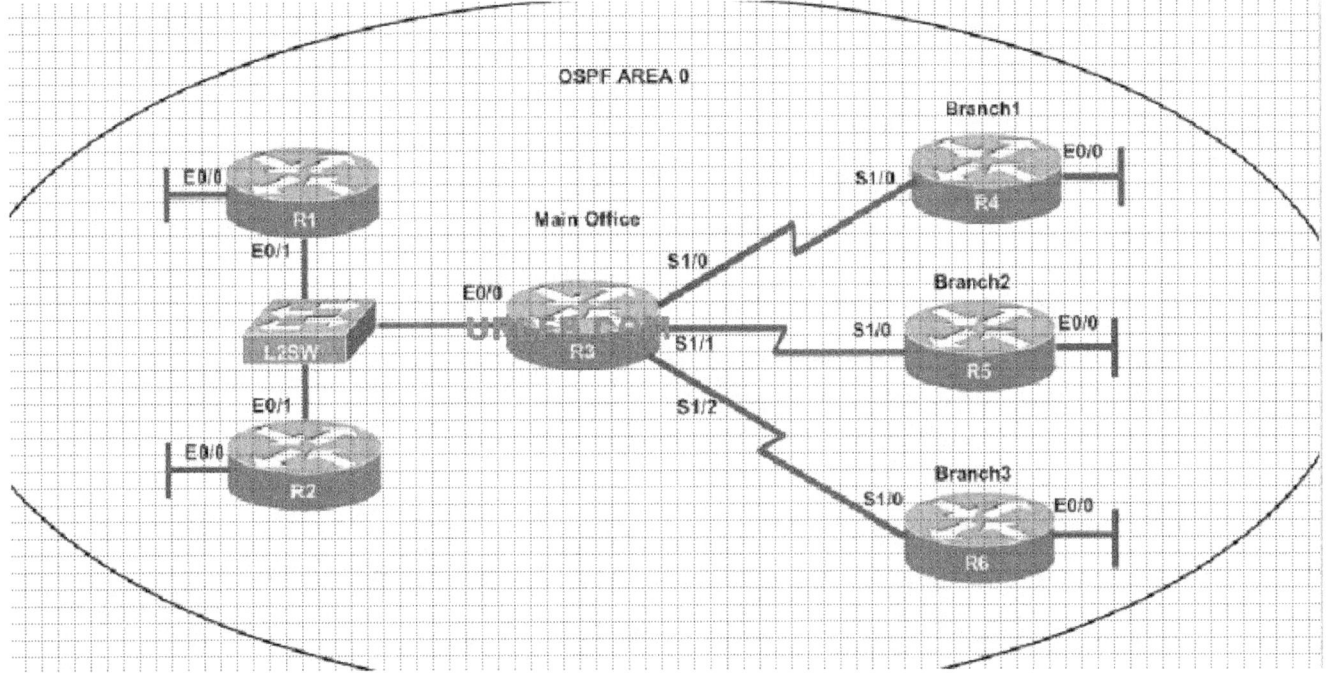

An OSPF neighbor adjacency is not formed between R3 in the main office and R6 in the Branch3 office. What is causing the problem?

A. There is an area ID mismatch

B. There is a PPP authentication issue; the username is not configured on R3 and R6

C. There is an OSPF hello and dead interval mismatch

D. The R3 router ID is configured on R6

24. What are benefits of private IPv4 IP addresses? Choose 2 options

A. They eliminate the necessity for NAT policies.

B. They can be assigned to devices without Internet connections.

C. They are less costly than public IP addresses.

D. They eliminate duplicate IP conflicts.

25. Refer to the exhibit.

*00:00:39: %LINEPROTO-5-UPDOWN: Line protocol on Interface Vlan1, changed state to down*

00:00:40: %SPANTREE-5-EXTENDED_SYSID: Extended SysId enabled for type vlan
00:00:42: %SYS-5-CONFIG_I: Configured from memory by console
00:00:42: %SYS-5-RESTART: System restarted–
Cisco IOS Software, C2960 Software (C2960-LANBASEK9-M), Version 12.2(25)SEE2, RELEASE SOFTWARE (fc.1)
Copyright(c) 1986-2006 by Cisco Systems, Inc.
Compiled Fri 28-Jul-06 11:57 by yenanh
00:00:44: %LINK-5-CHANGED: Interface Vlan1, changed state to administratively down
00:00:44: %LINK-3-UPDOWN: Interface FastEthernet0/1, changed state to up
00:00:44: %LINK-3-UPDOWN: Interface FastEthernet0/2, changed state to up
00:00:44: %LINK-3-UPDOWN: Interface FastEthernet0/11, changed state to up
00:00:45: %LINEPROTO-5-UPDOWN: Line protocol on Interface FastEthernet0/1, changed state to up
00:00:45: %LINEPROTO-5-UPDOWN: Line protocol on Interface FastEthernet0/2, changed state to up
00:00:45: %LINEPROTO-5-UPDOWN: Line protocol on Interface FastEthernet0/11, changed state to up
00:00:48: %LINK-3-UPDOWN: Interface FastEthernet0/12, changed state to up
00:00:49: %LINEPROTO-5-UPDOWN: Line protocol on Interface FastEthernet0/12, changed state to up

**Which of these statements correctly describes the state of the switch once the boot process has been completed? choose 2 options**

A. As FastEthernet0/12 will be the last to come up, it will be blocked by STP.

B. The switch will need a different IOS code in order to support VLANs and ST?.

C. Remote access management of this switch will not be possible without configuration change.

D. More VLANs will need to be created for this switch.

**26. Which statements about IPv6 and routing protocols are true? Choose 2 options**

A. Link-local addresses are used to form routing adjacencies.

B. EIGRPv3 was developed to support IPv6 routing.

C. OSPFv3 was developed to support IPv6 routing.

D. Loopback addresses are used to form routing adjacencies.

E. EIGRP, OSPF, and BGP are the only routing protocols that support IPv6.

**27. Which command would you configure globally on a Cisco device that would allow you to view directly connected other Cisco devices? choose 1 options**

A. cdp run

28. Which exec command can you enter to verify that a BGP connection to a remote device is established?choose 1 options

A. show ip bgp summary

29. What will happen if a private IP address is assigned to a public interface connected to an ISP?choose 1 options

A. Addresses in a private range will not be routed on the Internet backbone.

B. A conflict of IP addresses happens, because other public routers can use the same range.

C. The NAT process will be used to translate this address to a valid IP address.

D. Only the ISP router will have the capability to access the public network.

30. If the primary root bridge experiences a power loss, which switch takes over? choose 1 options

A. switch 0040.0??0.90C5

B. switch 0004.9A1A.C182

C. switch 00E0.F90B.6BE3

D. switch 00E0.F726.3DC6

31. Which statements about IPv6 prefixes are true?
choose 3 options

A. FEC0::/10 is used for IPv6 broadcast.

B. FE80::/10 is used for link-local unicast

C. FC00::/7 is used in private networks.

D. FF00::/8 is used for IPv6 multicast.

E. FE80::/8 is used for link-local unicast.

32. Which command can you enter to verify that a BGP connection to a remote device is established?choose 1 options

A. show ip route

B. show ip bgp paths

C. show ip bgp summary

D. show ip community-list

Answer: B

33. A network administrator is troubleshooting an EIGRP problem on a router and needs to confirm the IP addresses of the devices with which the router has established adjacency. The retransmit interval and the queue counts for the adjacent routers also need to be checked. What command will display the required information?choose 1 options

A. Router# show ip eigrp adjacency

B. Router# show ip eigrp neighbors

C. Router# show ip eigrp interfaces

D. Router# show ip eigrp topology

Answer: B

34. Which feature builds a FIB and an adjacency table to expedite packet forwarding? choose 1 options

A. Cisco Express Forwarding

B. fast switching

C. process switching

D. cut through

Answer: A

35. Refer to the exhibit

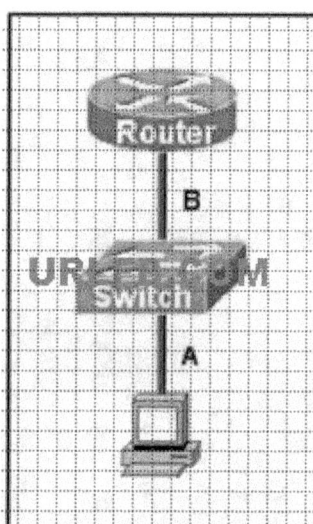

The two connected ports on the switch are not turning orange or green
Which three would be the most effective steps to troubleshoot this physical layer problem? (Choose three)

A. Reseat all cables

B. Ensure the switch has power

C. Ensure that the Ethernet encapsulations match on the interconnected router and switch ports

D. Ensure cable A is plugged into a trunk port

E. Reboot all of the devices

F. Ensure that cables A and B are straight-through cables.

36. A router has learned three possible routes that could be used to reach a destination network. One route is from EIGRP and has a composite metric of 20514560. Another route is from OSPF with a metric of 782. The last is from RIPv2 and has a metric of 4. Which route or routes will the router install in the routing table?choose 1 options

A. the EIGRP route

B. the RIPv2 route

C. all three routes

D. the OSPF and RIPv2 routes

E. the OSPF route

37. Which circumstances can cause a GRE tunnel to be in an up/down state? choose 3 options

A. A valid route to the destination address is missing from the routing table.

B. The tunnel address is routed through the tunnel itself.

C. The tunnel interface is down.

D. The ISP is blocking the traffic.

E. The tunnel interface IP address is misconfigured.

38. Which statement about LLDP is true?
choose 1 options

A. It is a Cisco proprietary protocol.

B. It is configured in global configuration mode.

C. The LLDP update frequency is a fixed value.

D. It runs over the transport layer.

**39. In which formats can the IPv6 address fd15:0db8:0000:0000:0700:0003:400F:572B be written? choose 2 options**

A. fd15:0db8::7:3:4F:527B

B. fd15:db8:0::700:3:4F:527B

C. fd15:0db8:0000:0000:700:3:400F:527B

D. fd15::db8::700:3:400F:527B

E. fd15:db8::700:3:400F:572B

**40. Which statements correctly describe steps in the OSI data encapsulation process? choose 2 options**

A. The transport layer divides a data stream into segments and may add reliability and flow control information.

B. Packets are created when the network layer adds Layer 3 addresses and control information to a segment.

C. The presentation layer translates bits into voltages for transmission across the physical link.

D. Packets are created when the network layer encapsulates a frame with source and destination host addresses and protocol-related control information.

E. The data link layer adds physical source and destination addresses and an FCS to the segment.

**41. Which statements about using leased lines for your WAN infrastructure are true? choose 2 options**

A. Leased lines provide highly flexible bandwidth scaling.
B. Leased lines require little installation and maintenance expertise.
C. Leased lines provide inexpensive WAN access.

D. Leased lines with sufficient bandwidth can avoid latency between endpoints.

E. Multiple leased lines can share a router interface.

**42. What is the result of issuing the frame-relay map ip 192.168.1.2 202 broadcast command?**

A. defines the destination IP address that is used in all broadcast packets on DCLI 202
B. defines the source IP address that is used in all broadcast packets on DCLI 202
C. defines the DLCI on which packets from the 192.168.1.2 IP address are received
D. defines the DLCI that is used for all packets that are sent to the 192.168.1.2 IP address

Answer: D
Explanation:
This command identifies the DLCI that should be used for all packets destined to the 192.168.1.2
address. In this case, DLCI 202 should be used.

43. Which PPP subprotocol negotiates authentication options?

A. NCP
B. ISDN
C. SLIP
D. LCP
E. DLCI

Answer:    D
Explanation:
The PPP Link Control Protocol (LCP) is documented in RFC 1661. LPC negotiates link and PPP parameters to dynamically configure the data link layer of a PPP connection. Common LCP options include the PPP MRU, the authentication protocol, compression of PPP header fields, callback, and multilink options.

44. What are two characteristics of Frame Relay point-to-point subinterfaces? (Choose two.)

A. They create split-horizon issues.
B. They require a unique subnet within a routing domain.
C. They emulate leased lines.
D. They are ideal for full-mesh topologies.
E. They require the use of NBMA options when using OSPF.

Answer:  BC
Explanation:
Subinterfaces are used for point to point frame relay connections, emulating virtual point to point leased lines. Each subinterface requires a unique IP address/subnet. Remember, you can not assign multiple interfaces in a router that belong to the same IP subnet.

45. What command is used to verify the DLCI destination address in a Frame Relay static configuration?

A. show frame-relay pvc
B. show frame-relay lmi
C. show frame-relay map
D. show frame relay end-to-end

Answer: C
Explanation:
Sample "show frame-relay map" output:
R1#sh frame mapSerial0/0 (up): ip 10.4.4.1 dlci 401(0x191,0x6410), dynamic,broadcast,, status defined, activeSerial0/0 (up): ip 10.4.4.3 dlci 403(0x193,0x6430), dynamic,broadcast,, status defined, activeSerial0/0 (up): ip 10.4.4.4 dlci 401(0x191,0x6410), static,CISCO, status defined, active

46. What is the purpose of Inverse ARP?

A. to map a known IP address to a MAC address
B. to map a known DLCI to a MAC address
C. to map a known MAC address to an IP address
D. to map a known DLCI to an IP address
E. to map a known IP address to a SPID
F. to map a known SPID to a MAC address

Answer: D
Explanation:
Dynamic address mapping relies on the Frame Relay Inverse Address Resolution Protocol (Inverse ARP), defined by RFC 1293, to resolve a next hop network protocol (IP) address to a local DLCI value. The Frame Relay router sends out Inverse ARP requests on its Frame Relay PVC to discover the protocol address of the remote device connected to the Frame Relay network. The responses to the Inverse ARP requests are used to populate an address-to-DLCI mapping table on the Frame
Relay router or access server. The router builds and maintains this address-to- DLCI mapping table, which contains all resolved Inverse ARP requests, including both dynamic and static mapping entries.

47. Two routers named Atlanta and Brevard are connected via their serial interfaces as illustrated, but they are unable to communicate. The Atlanta router is known to have the correct configuration.

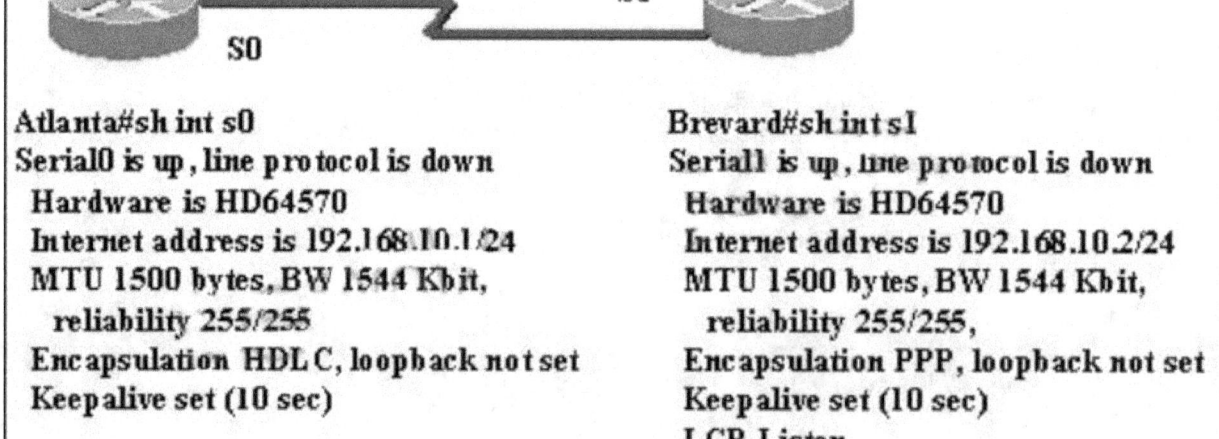

Given the partial configurations, identify the fault on the Brevard router that is causing the lack of connectivity.
A. incompatible IP address
B. insufficient bandwidth
C. incorrect subnet mask
D. incompatible encapsulation
E. link reliability too low
F. IPCP closed

**Answer: D**
**Explanation:**
The correct explanation should be that the Atlanta router is usng HDLC while the Brevard is using
PPP. These need to match on both ends.

48. Refer to the exhibit. The company uses EIGRP as the routing protocol. What path will packets take from a host on the 192.168.10.192/26 network to a host on the LAN attached to router R1?

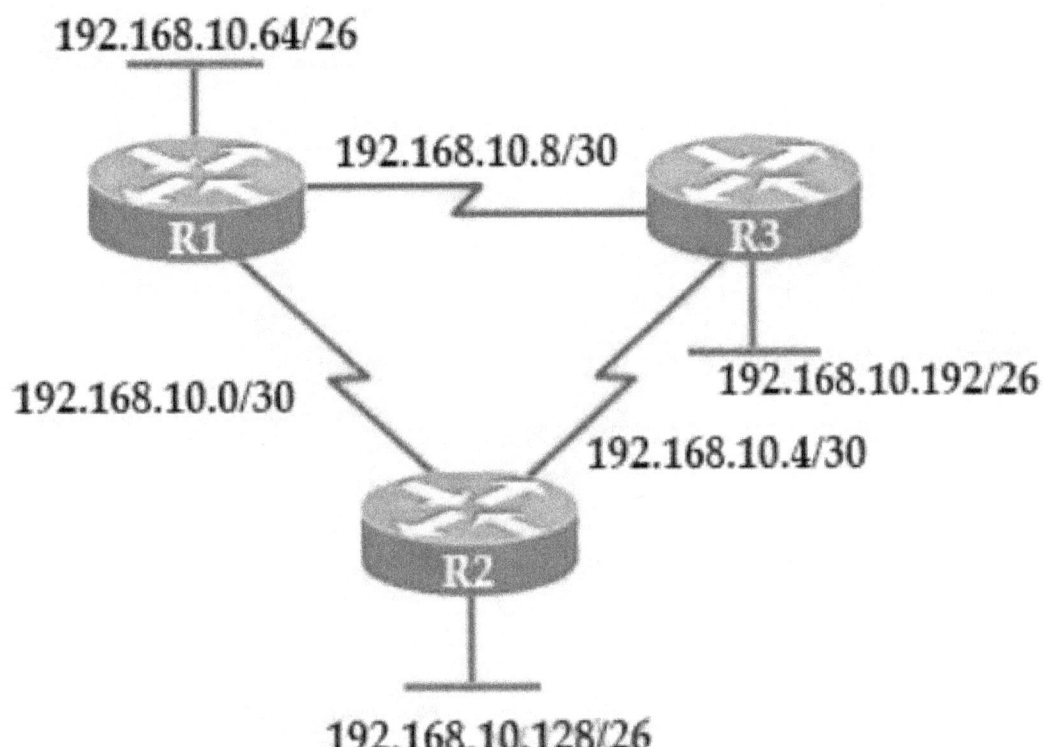

```
R3# show ip route
Gateway of last resort is not set
192.168.10.0/24 is variably subnetted, 6 subnets, 2 masks
D   192.168.10.64/26 [90/2195456] via 192.168.10.9, 00:03:31, Serial0/0
D   192.168.10.0/30 [90/2681856] via 192.168.10.9, 00:03:31, Serial0/0
C   192.168.10.4/30 is directly connected, Serial 0/1
C   192.168.10.8/30 is directly connected, Serial 0/0
C   192.168.10.192/26 is directly connected, FastEthernet0/0
D   192.168.10.128/26 [90/2195456] via 192.168.10.5, 00:03 31, Serial 0/1
```

A. The path of the packets will be R3 to R2 to R1.
B. The path of the packets will be R3 to R1 to R2.
C. The path of the packets will be both R3 to R2 to R1 AND R3 to R1.
D. The path of the packets will be R3 to R1.

**Answer:   D**
**Explanation:**
Host on the LAN attached to router R1 belongs to 192.168.10.64/26 subnet. From the output of the routing table of R3 we learn this network can be reach via 192.168.10.9, which is an IP address in 192.168.10.8/30 network (the network between R1 & R3) -> packets destined for 192.168.10.64 will be routed from R3 -> R1 -> LAN on R1.

**49. How does using the service password-encryption command on a router provide additional security?**

A. by encrypting all passwords passing through the router
B. by encrypting passwords in the plain text configuration file
C. by requiring entry of encrypted passwords for access to the device
D. by configuring an MD5 encrypted key to be used by routing protocols to validate routing exchanges
E. by automatically suggesting encrypted passwords for use in configuring the router

**Answer: B**
**Explanation:**
By using this command, all the (current and future) passwords are encrypted. This command is primarily useful for keeping unauthorized individuals from viewing your password in your configuration file

**50. Refer to the exhibit. Switch port FastEthernet 0/24 on ALSwitch1 will be used to create an IEEE 802.1Q-compliant trunk to another switch. Based on the output shown, what is the reason the trunk does not form, even though the proper cabling has been attached?**

```
ALSwitch1# show running-config
«output omitted»
interface FastEthernet0/24 no ip address
«output omitted»
ALSwitch1# show interfaces FastEthernet0/24 switchport
Name: Fa0/24
Switchport: Enable
Administrative Mode: static access
Operation Mode: static access
Administrative Trunking Encapsulation: dot1q
Operation Trunking Encapsulation: native
Negotiation of Trunking: Off
Access Mode VLAN: 1 (default)
Trunking Native Mode VLAN: 1 (default)
Voice VLAN: none
Administrative private-vlan host-association: none
Administrative private-vlan mapping: none
Operation private-vlan: none
Trunking VLANs Enabled: ALL
Pruning VLANs Enabled: 2-1001
Capture Mode Disabled
Capture VLANs Allowed: ALL

Protected: false

Voice VLAN: none (Inactive)
Aplliance trust: none
```

A. VLANs have not been created yet.
B. An IP address must be configured for the port.
C. The port is currently configured for access mode.
D. The correct encapsulation type has not been configured.
E. The no shutdown command has not been entered for the port.

Answer: C
Explanation:
According to the output shown the switchport (layer 2 Switching) is enabled and the port is in access mode. To make a trunk link the port should configured as a trunk port, not an access port, by using the following command: (Config-if)#switchport mode trunk

**51. Refer to the exhibit. In the Frame Relay network, which IP addresses would be assigned to the interfaces with point-to- point PVCs?**

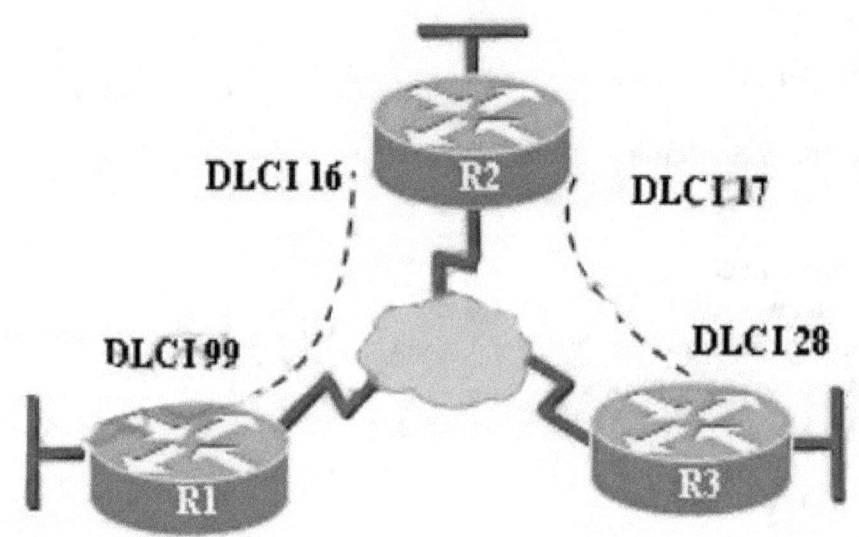

A. DLCI 16: 192.168.10.1 /24
DLCI 17: 192.168.10.1 /24
DLCI 99: 192.168.10.2 /24
DLCI 28: 192.168.10.3 /24

B. DLCI 16: 192.168.10.1 /24
DLCI 17: 192.168.11.1 /24
DLCI 99: 192.168.12.1 /24
DLCI 28: 192.168.13.1 /24

C. DLCI 16: 192.168.10.1 /24
DLCI 17: 192.168.11.1 /24
DLCI 99: 192.168.10.2 /24
DLCI 28: 192.168.11.2 /24

D. DLCI 16: 192.168.10.1 /24
DLCI 17: 192.168.10.2 /24
DLCI 99: 192.168.10.3 /24
DLCI 28: 192.168.10.4 /24

**Answer: C**
**Explanation:**
With point to point PVC, each connection needs to be in a separate subnet. The R2-R1 connection (DLCI 16 to 99) would have each router within the same subnet. Similarly, the R3-R1 connection would also be in the same subnet, but it must be in a different one than the R2-R1 connection.

**52. Refer to the exhibit. A new subnet with 60 hosts has been added to the network. Which subnet address should this network use to provide enough usable addresses while wasting the fewest addresses?**

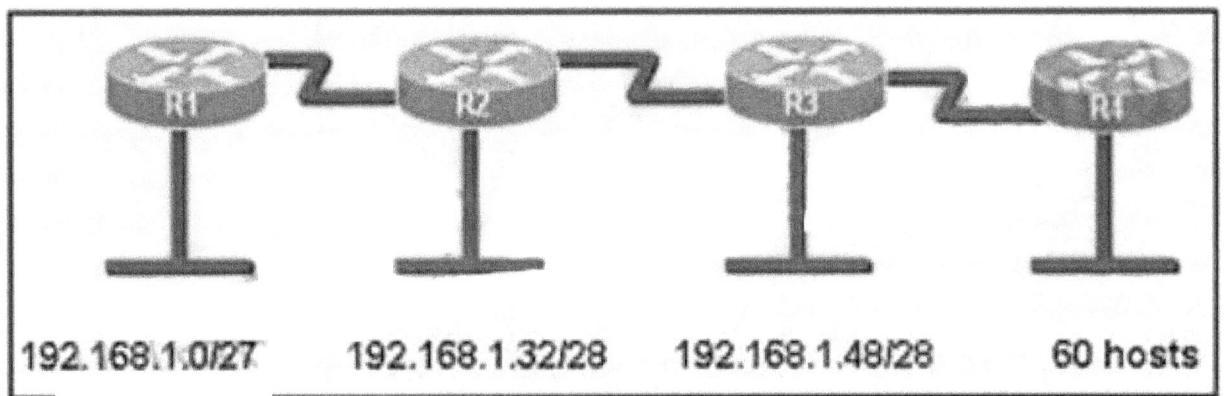

A. 192.168.1.56/26
B. 192.168.1.56/27
C. 192.168.1.64/26
D. 192.168.1.64/27

Answer: C
Explanation:
A subnet with 60 host is 2*2*2*2*2*2 = 64 -2 == 62
6 bits needed for hosts part. Therefore subnet bits are 2 bits (8-6) in fourth octet.
8bits+ 8bits+ 8bits + 2bits = /26
/26 bits subnet is 24bits + 11000000 = 24bits + 192
256 -192 = 64
0 - 63
64 - 127

53. Refer to the exhibit. All of the routers in the network are configured with the ip subnet-zero command. Which network addresses should be used for Link A and Network A? (Choose two.)

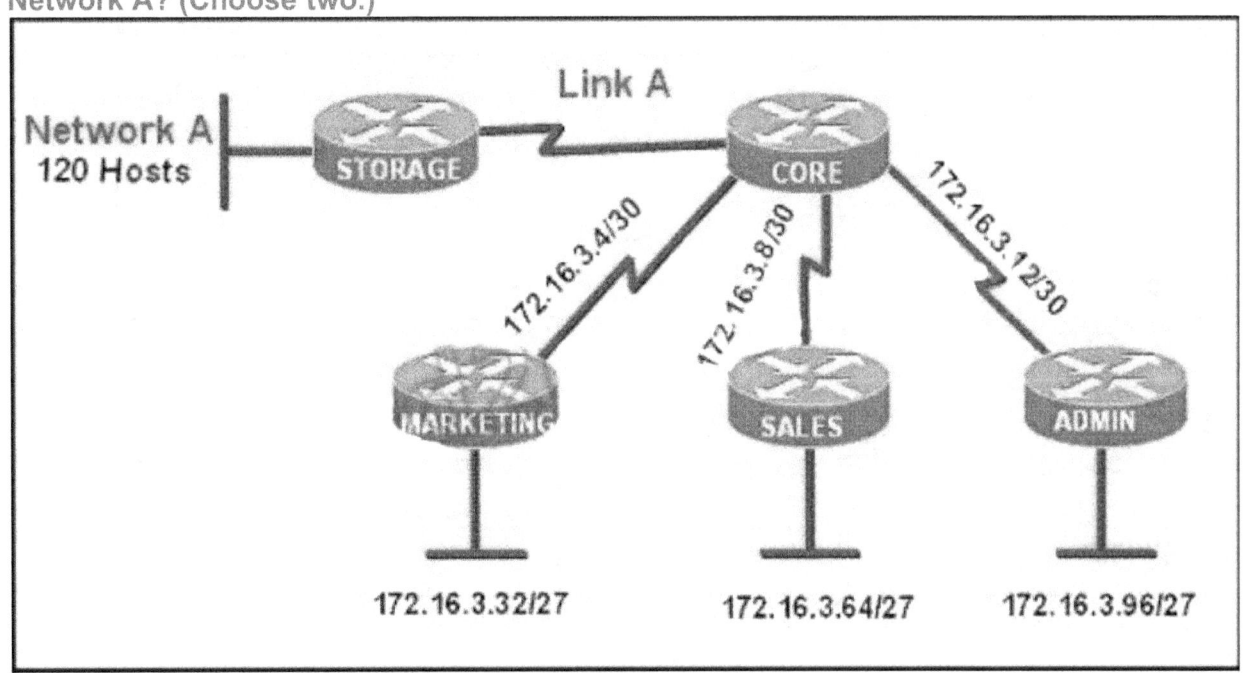

A. Network A - 172.16.3.48/26
B. Network A - 172.16.3.128/25
C. Network A - 172.16.3.192/26
D. Link A - 172.16.3.0/30
E. Link A - 172.16.3.40/30
F. Link A - 172.16.3.112/30

**Answer: BD**
**Explanation:**
Only a /30 is needed for the point to point link and sine the use of the ip subnet-zero was used, 172.16.3.0/30 is valid. Also, a /25 is required for 120 hosts and again 172.16.3.128/25 is the best, valid option.

54. A router has learned three possible routes that could be used to reach a destination network. One route is from EIGRP and has a composite metric of 20514560. Another route is from OSPF with a metric of 782. The last is from RIPv2 and has a metric of 4. Which route or routes will the router install in the routing table?

A. the OSPF route
B. the EIGRP route
C. the RIPv2 route
D. all three routes
E. the OSPF and RIPv2 routes

**Answer: B**
**Explanation:**
When one route is advertised by more than one routing protocol, the router will choose to use the routing protocol which has lowest Administrative Distance. The Administrative Distances of popular routing protocols are listed below:

| Route Source | Administrative Distance |
|---|---|
| Directly Connected | 0 |
| Static | 1 |
| EIGRP | 90 |
| EIGRP Summary route | 5 |
| OSPF | 110 |
| RIP | 120 |

55. A network administrator needs to allow only one Telnet connection to a router. For anyone viewing the configuration and issuing the show run command, the password for Telnet access should be encrypted. Which set of commands will accomplish this task?

A. service password-encryption
access-list 1 permit 192.168.1.0 0.0.0.255
line vty 0 4
login
password cisco
access-class 1

B. enable password secret
line vty 0
login
password cisco

C. service password-encryption
line vty 1
login
password cisco

D. service password-encryption
line vty 0 4
login
password cisco

Answer: C
Explanation:
Only one VTY connection is allowed which is exactly what's requested.
Incorrect answer: command.
line vty0 4 would enable all 5 vty connections.

56. Refer to the exhibit. The speed of all serial links is E1 and the speed of all Ethernet links is 100 Mb/s. A static route will be established on the Manchester router to direct traffic toward the Internet over the most direct path available. What configuration on the Manchester router will establish a route toward the Internet for traffic that originates from workstations on the Manchester LAN?

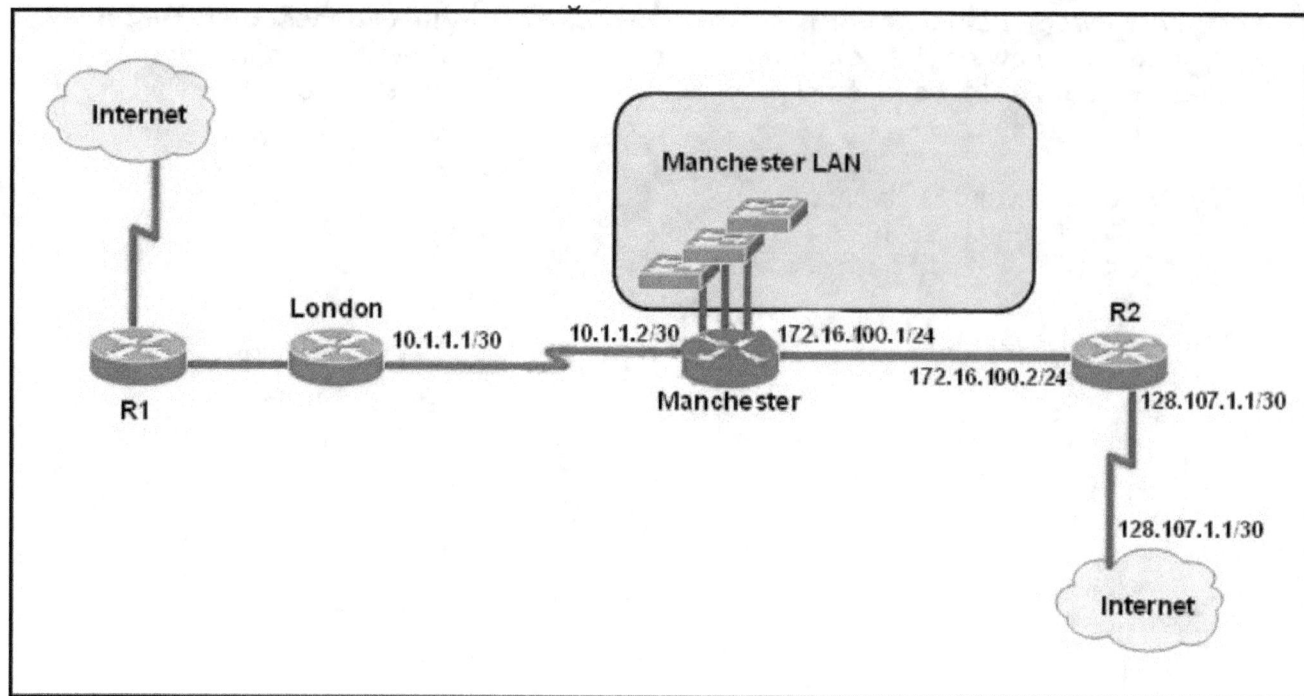

A. ip route 0.0.0.0 255.255.255.0 172.16.100.2
B. ip route 0.0.0.0 0.0.0.0 128.107.1.1
C. ip route 0.0.0.0 255.255.255.252 128.107.1.1
D. ip route 0.0.0.0 0.0.0.0 172.16.100.1
E. ip route 0.0.0.0 0.0.0.0 172.16.100.2
F. ip route 0.0.0.0 255.255.255.255 172.16.100.2

**Answer: E**
**Explanation:**
We use default routing to send packets with a remote destination network not in the routing table to the next-hop router. You should generally only use default routing on stub networks--those with only one exit path out of the network.
According to exhibit, all traffic towards Internet that originates from workstations should forward to
Router R1.
Syntax for default route is:
ip route <Remote_Network> <Netmask> <Next_Hop_Address>.

**57. Refer to the exhibit. The network administrator must establish a route by which London workstations can forward traffic to the Manchester workstations. What is the simplest way to accomplish this?**

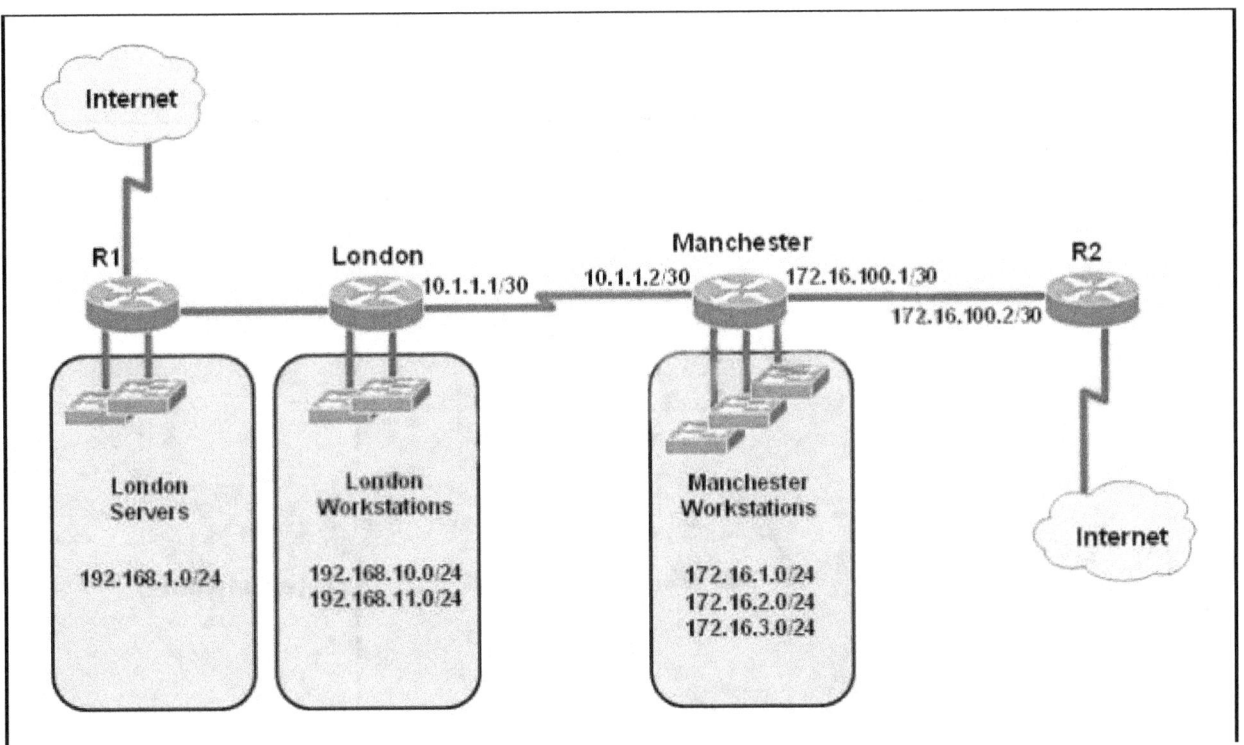

A. Configure a dynamic routing protocol on London to advertise all routes to Manchester.

B. Configure a dynamic routing protocol on London to advertise summarized routes to Manchester.

C. Configure a dynamic routing protocol on Manchester to advertise a default route to the London router.

D. Configure a static default route on London with a next hop of 10.1.1.1.

E. Configure a static route on London to direct all traffic destined for 172.16.0.0/22 to 10.1.1.2.

F. Configure Manchester to advertise a static default route to London.

**Answer: E**
Explanation:
This static route will allow for communication to the Manchester workstations and it is better to use this more specific route than a default route as traffic destined to the Internet will then not go out the London Internet connection.

**58. Refer to the exhibit. The network administrator requires easy configuration options and minimal routing protocol traffic. What two options provide adequate**

routing table information for traffic that passes between the two routers and satisfy the requests of the network administrator? (Choose two.)

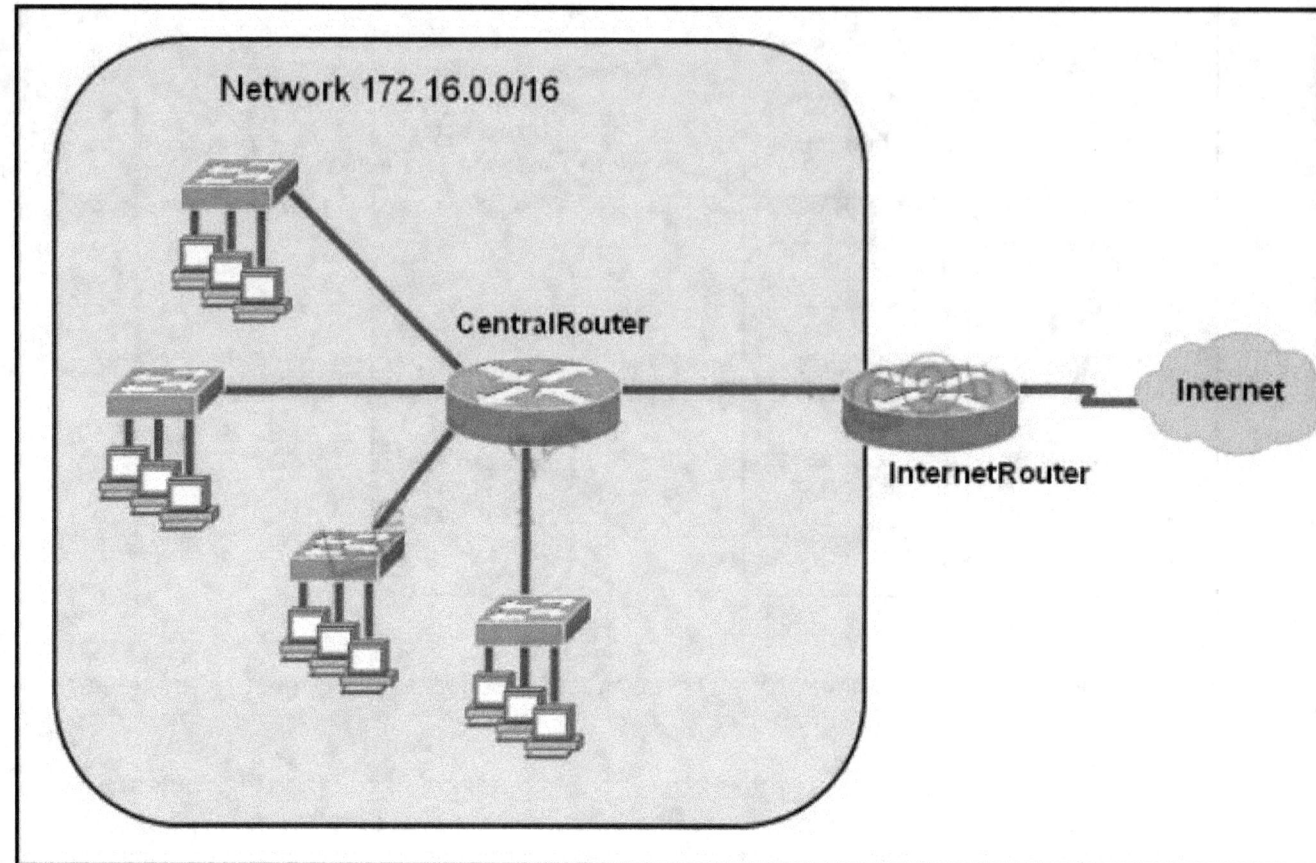

A. a dynamic routing protocol on InternetRouter to advertise all routes to CentralRouter.

B. a dynamic routing protocol on InternetRouter to advertise summarized routes to CentralRouter.

C. a static route on InternetRouter to direct traffic that is destined for 172.16.0.0/16 to CentralRouter.

D. a dynamic routing protocol on CentralRouter to advertise all routes to InternetRouter.
E. a dynamic routing protocol on CentralRouter to advertise summarized routes to InternetRouter.

F. a static, default route on CentralRouter that directs traffic to InternetRouter.

**Answer: CF**
**Explanation:**

The use of static routes will provide the necessary information for connectivity while producing no routing traffic overhead.

## 59. What is the effect of using the service password-encryption command?

A. Only the enable password will be encrypted.
B. Only the enable secret password will be encrypted.
C. Only passwords configured after the command has been entered will be encrypted.
D. It will encrypt the secret password and remove the enable secret password from the configuration.
E. It will encrypt all current and future passwords.

Answer:    E
Explanation:
Enable vty, console, AUX passwords are configured on the Cisco device. Use the show run command to show most passwords in clear text. If the service password-encryption is used, all the passwords are encrypted. As a result, the security of device access is improved.

## 60. Refer to the exhibit. What is the effect of the configuration that is shown?

```
line vty 0 4
  password 7 030752180500
  login
  transport input ssh
```

A. It configures SSH globally for all logins.
B. It tells the router or switch to try to establish an SSh connection first and if that fails to use Telnet.
C. It configures the virtual terminal lines with the password 030752180500.
D. It configures a Cisco network device to use the SSH protocol on incoming communications via the
virtual terminal ports.
E. It allows seven failed login attempts before the VTY lines are temporarily shutdown.

Answer: D
Explanation:
Secure Shell (SSH) is a protocol which provides a secure remote access connection to network devices. Communication between the client and server is encrypted in both SSH version 1 and SSH version 2. If you want to prevent non-SSH connections, add the "transport input ssh" command under the lines to limit the router to SSH connections only. Straight (non-SSH) Telnets are refused. www.cisco.com/warp/public/707/ssh.shtml

## 61. Refer to the exhibit. A junior network administrator was given the task of configuring port security on SwitchA to allow only PC_A to access the switched network through port fa0/1. If any other device is detected, the port is to drop frames

from this device. The administrator configured the interface and tested it with successful pings from PC_A to RouterA, and then observes the output from these two show commands. Which two of these changes are necessary for SwitchA to meet the requirements? (Choose two.)

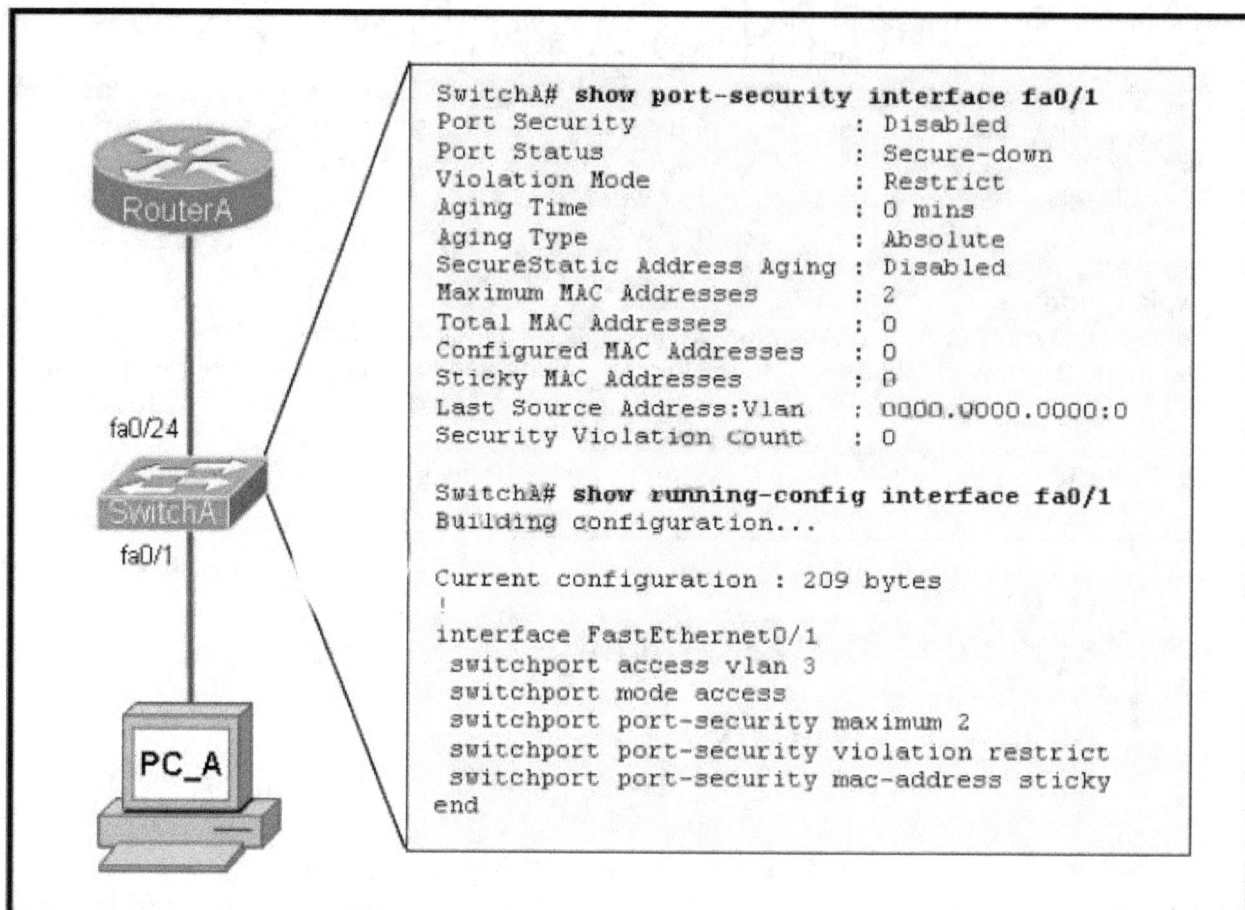

A. Port security needs to be globally enabled.
B. Port security needs to be enabled on the interface.
C. Port security needs to be configured to shut down the interface in the event of a violation.
D. Port security needs to be configured to allow only one learned MAC address.
E. Port security interface counters need to be cleared before using the show command.
F. The port security configuration needs to be saved to NVRAM before it can become active.

Answer: BD
Explanation:
From the output we can see that port security is disabled so this needs to be enabled. Also, the maximum number of devices is set to 2 so this needs to be just one if we want the single host to have access and nothing else.

62. Refer to the exhibit. When running OSPF, what would cause router A not to form an adjacency with router B?

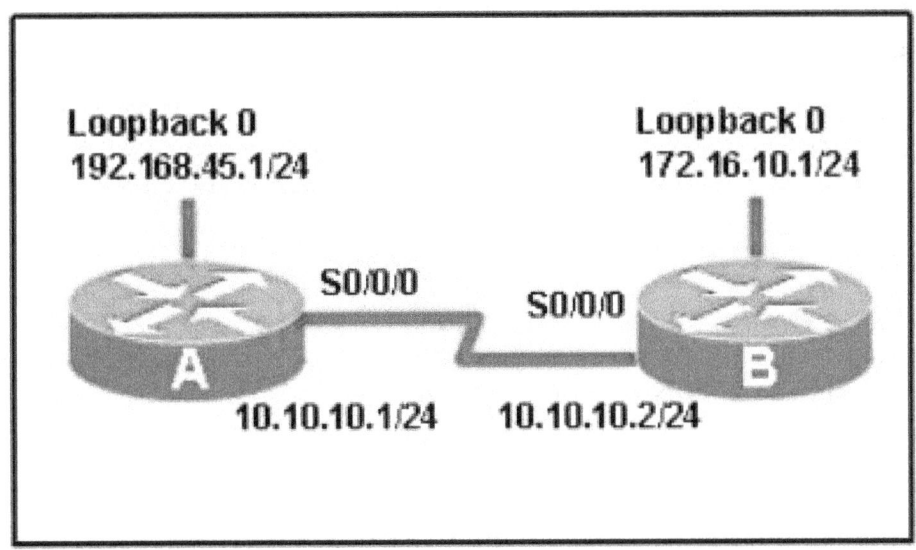

A. The loopback addresses are on different subnets.
B. The values of the dead timers on the routers are different.
C. Route summarization is enabled on both routers.
D. The process identifier on router A is different than the process identifier on router B.

Answer: B
Explanation:
To form an adjacency (become neighbor), router A & B must have the same Hello interval, Dead interval and AREA number.s

63. Which two of these statements are true of IPv6 address representation? (Choose two.)

A. There are four types of IPv6 addresses: unicast, multicast, anycast, and broadcast.
B. A single interface may be assigned multiple IPv6 addresses of any type.
C. Every IPv6 interface contains at least one loopback address.
D. The first 64 bits represent the dynamically created interface ID.
E. Leading zeros in an IPv6 16 bit hexadecimal field are mandatory.

Answer: BC
Explanation:
Leading zeros in IPv6 are optional do that 05C7 equals 5C7 and 0000 equals 0 -> D is not correct.

64. Which set of commands is recommended to prevent the use of a hub in the access layer?

A. switch(config-if)#switchport mode trunk
switch(config-if)#switchport port-security maximum 1

B. switch(config-if)#switchport mode trunk
switch(config-if)#switchport port-security mac-address 1

C. switch(config-if)#switchport mode access
switch(config-if)#switchport port-security maximum 1

D. switch(config-if)#switchport mode access
switch(config-if)#switchport port-security mac-address 1

Answer: C
Explanation:
This question is to examine the layer 2 security configuration. In order to satisfy the requirements of this question, you should perform the following configurations in the interface mode: First, configure the interface mode as the access mode Second, enable the port security and set the maximum number of connections to 1.

65. What is known as "one-to-nearest" addressing in IPv6?

A. global unicast
B. anycast
C. multicast
D. unspecified address

Answer: B
Explanation:
IPv6 Anycast addresses are used for one-to-nearest communication, meaning an Anycast address
is used by a device to send data to one specific recipient (interface) that is the closest out of a
group of recipients (interfaces).

66. What is the first 24 bits in a MAC address called?

A. NIC
B. BIA
C. OUI
D. VAI

Answer: C
Explanation:
An Organizationally Unique Identifier (OUI) is a 24-bit number that uniquely identifies a vendor, manufacturer, or other organization globally or worldwide. They are used as the first 24 nits of the MAC address to uniquely identify a particular piece of equipment.

67. Refer to the exhibit. Which subnet mask will place all hosts on Network B in the same subnet with the least amount of wasted addresses?

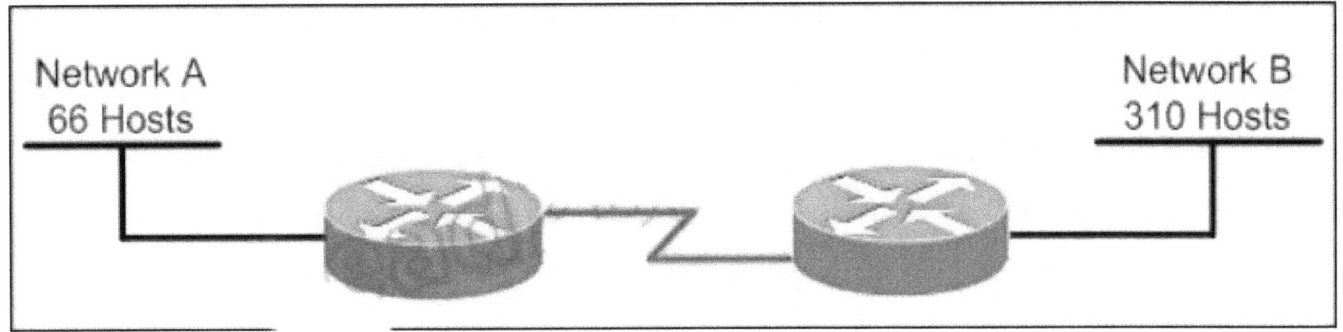

A. 255.255.255.0
B. 255.255.254.0
C. 255.255.252.0
D. 255.255.248.0

Answer: B
Explanation:
310 hosts < 512 = 29 -> We need a subnet mask of 9 bits 0 -> 1111 1111.1111 1111.1111 1110.0000 0000 -> 255.255.254.0

68. Refer to the exhibit. What is the most appropriate summarization for these routes?

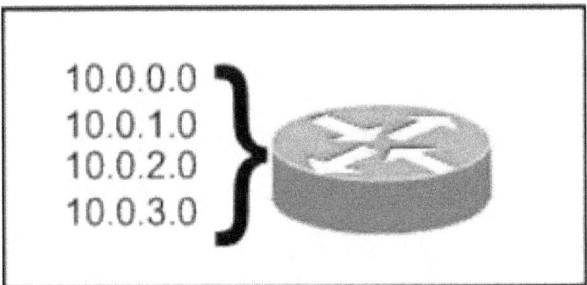

A. 10.0.0.0 /21
B. 10.0.0.0 /22
C. 10.0.0.0 /23
D. 10.0.0.0 /24

Answer: B
Explanation:
The 10.0.0.0/22 subnet mask will include the 10.0.0.0, 10.0.1.0, 10.0.2.0, and 10.0.3.0 networks, and only those four networks.

69. What is the difference between a CSU/DSU and a modem?

A. A CSU/DSU converts analog signals from a router to a leased line; a modem converts analog signals from a router to a leased line.

B. A CSU/DSU converts analog signals from a router to a phone line; a modem converts digital signals from a router to a leased line.

C. A CSU/DSU converts digital signals from a router to a phone line; a modem converts analog signals from a router to a phone line.

D. A CSU/DSU converts digital signals from a router to a leased line; a modem converts digital signals from a router to a phone line.

**Answer: D**
**Explanation:**
CSU/DSU is used to convert digital signals from a router to a network circuit such as a T1, while a modem is used to convert digital signals over a regular POTS line.

*70.* Which two are features of IPv6? (Choose two.)
A. anycast
B. broadcast
C. multicast
D. podcast
E. allcast

**Answer: AC**
**Explanation:**
IPv6 addresses are classified by the primary addressing and routing methodologies common in networkinG. unicast addressing, anycast addressing, and multicast addressing.

**71. Which two are advantages of static routing when compared to dynamic routing? (Choose two.)**

A. Configuration complexity decreases as network size increases.
B. Security increases because only the network administrator may change the routing table.
C. Route summarization is computed automatically by the router.
D. Routing tables adapt automatically to topology changes.
E. An efficient algorithm is used to build routing tables, using automatic updates.
F. Routing updates are automatically sent to neighbors.
G. Routing traffic load is reduced when used in stub network links.

**Answer: BG**
**Explanation:**
Since static routing is a manual process, it can be argued that it is more secure (and more prone to human errors) since the network administrator will need to make changes to the routing table directly. Also, in stub networks where there is only a single uplink connection, the load is reduced as stub routers just need a single static default route, instead of many routes that all have the same next hop IP address.

**72. A network administrator needs to configure port security on a switch. Which two statements are true? (Choose two.)**

A. The network administrator can apply port security to dynamic access ports.
B. The network administrator can apply port security to EtherChannels.
C. When dynamic MAC address learning is enabled on an interface, the switch can learn new addresses, up to the maximum defined.

D. The sticky learning feature allows the addition of dynamically learned addresses to the running configuration.
E. The network administrator can configure static secure or sticky secure MAC addresses in the voice VLAN.

**Answer: CD**
**Explanation:**
Follow these guidelines when configuring port security:
+ Port security can only be configured on static access ports, trunk ports, or 802.1Q tunnel ports.
+ A secure port cannot be a dynamic access port.
+ A secure port cannot be a destination port for Switched Port Analyzer (SPAN). + A secure port cannot belong to a Fast EtherChannel or Gigabit EtherChannel port group. + You cannot configure static secure or sticky secure MAC addresses on a voice VLAN. + When you enable port security on an interface that is also configured with a voice VLAN, you must set the maximum allowed secure addresses on the port to at least two. + If any type of port security is enabled on the access
VLAN, dynamic port security is automatically enabled on the voice VLAN.
+ When a voice VLAN is configured on a secure port that is also configured as a sticky secure port, all addresses seen on the voice VLAN are learned as dynamic secure addresses, and all addresses seen on the access VLAN (to which the port belongs) are learned as sticky secure addresses.
+ The switch does not support port security aging of sticky secure MAC addresses. + The protect and restrict options cannot be simultaneously enabled on an interface.http://www.cisco.com/en/US/docs/switches/lan/catalyst3550/software/release/12.1 _19_ea1/config uration/guide/swtrafc.html

**73. What are three features of the IPv6 protocol? (Choose three.)**

A. optional IPsec
B. autoconfiguration
C. no broadcasts
D. complicated header
E. plug-and-play
F. checksums

**Answer: BCE**
**Explanation:**
An important feature of IPv6 is that it allows plug and play option to the network devices by allowing them to configure themselves independently. It is possible to plug a node into an IPv6 network without requiring any human intervention. This feature was critical to allow network connectivity to an increasing number of mobile devices. This is accomplished by autoconfiguration.
IPv6 does not implement traditional IP broadcast, i.e. the transmission of a packet to all hosts on the attached link using a special broadcast address, and therefore does not define broadcast addresses. In IPv6, the same result can be achieved by sending a packet to the link-local all nodes multicast group at address ff02::1, which is analogous to IPv4 multicast to address 224.0.0.1.

## 74. Which command enables IPv6 forwarding on a Cisco router?

A. ipv6 local
B. ipv6 host
C. ipv6 unicast-routing
D. ipv6 neighbor

**Answer: C**
**Explanation:**
to enable IPv6 routing on the Cisco router use the following command: ipv6 unicast-routing
If this command is not recognized, your version of IOS does not support IPv6.

## 75. Which command encrypts all plaintext passwords?

A. Router# service password-encryption
B. Router(config)# password-encryption
C. Router(config)# service password-encryption
D. Router# password-encryption

**Answer: C**
**Explanation:**
The "service password-encryption" command allows you to encrypt all passwords on your router so they can not be easily guessed from your running-config. This command uses a very weak encryption because the router has to be very quickly decode the passwords for its operation. It is meant to prevent someone from looking over your shoulder and seeing the password, that is all. This is configured in global configuration mode.

## 76. You have been asked to come up with a subnet mask that will allow all three web servers to be on the same network while providing the maximum number of subnets. Which network address and subnet mask meet this requirement?

A. 192.168.252.0 255.255.255.252
B. 192.168.252.8 255.255.255.248
C. 192.168.252.8 255.255.255.252
D. 192.168.252.16 255.255.255.240
E. 192.168.252.16 255.255.255.252

**Answer: B**
**Explanation:**
A subnet mask of 255.255.255.248 will allow for up to 6 hosts to reside in this network. A subnet mask of 255.255.255.252 will allow for only 2 usable IP addresses, since we can not use the network or broadcast address.

## 77. Given an IP address 172.16.28.252 with a subnet mask of 255.255.240.0, what is the correct network address?

A. 172.16.16.0
B. 172.16.0.0

C. 172.16.24.0
D. 172.16.28.0

Answer: A
Explanation:
For this example, the network range is 172.16.16.1 - 172.16.31.254, the network address is 172.16.16.0 and the broadcast IP address is 172.16.31.255.

78. Which IPv6 address is the equivalent of the IPv4 interface loopback address 127.0.0.1?

A. ::1
B. ::
C. 2000::/3
D. 0::/10

Answer: A
Explanation:
In IPv6 the loopback address is written as, This is a 128bit number, with the first 127 bits being '0' and the 128th bit being '1'. It's just a single address, so could also be written as ::1/128.

79. You are working in a data center environment and are assigned the address range 10.188.31.0/23. You are asked to develop an IP addressing plan to allow the maximum number of subnets with as many as 30 hosts each. Which IP address range meets these requirements?

A. 10.188.31.0/26
B. 10.188.31.0/25
C. 10.188.31.0/28
D. 10.188.31.0/27
E. 10.188.31.0/29

Answer: D
Explanation:
Each subnet has 30 hosts < 32 = 25 so we need a subnet mask which has at least 5 bit 0s -> /27. Also the question requires the maximum number of subnets (which minimum the number of hosts- per-subnet) so /27 is the best choice -> .

80. Which parameter or parameters are used to calculate OSPF cost in Cisco routers?

A. Bandwidth
B. Bandwidth and Delay
C. Bandwidth, Delay, and MTU
D. Bandwidth, MTU, Reliability, Delay, and Load

Answer: A
Explanation:
The well-known formula to calculate OSPF cost is Cost = 108 / Bandwidth

**81. Why do large OSPF networks use a hierarchical design? (Choose three.)**

A. to decrease latency by increasing bandwidth
B. to reduce routing overhead
C. to speed up convergence
D. to confine network instability to single areas of the network
E. to reduce the complexity of router configuration
F. to lower costs by replacing routers with distribution layer switches

Answer: BCD
Explanation:
OSPF implements a two-tier hierarchical routing model that uses a core or backbone tier known as area zero (0). Attached to that backbone via area border routers (ABRs) are a number of secondary tier areas. The hierarchical approach is used to achieve the following:
Rapid convergence because of link and/or switch failures
Deterministic traffic recovery Scalable and manageable routing hierarchy, reduced routing overhead.

**82. Drag and Drop Question**

Drag the security features on the left to the specific security risks they help protect against on the right. (Not all options are used.)

| Security Features | Security Risks |
|---|---|
| access-group | remote access to device console |
| console password | access to the console 0 line |
| enable secret | access to connected networks or resources |
| CHAP authentication | viewing of passwords |
| VTY password | access to privileged mode |
| service password-encryption | |

Answer:Answer:

Drag the security features on the left to the specific security risks they help protect against on the right. (Not all options are used.)

| Left | Right |
|---|---|
| access-group | VTY password |
| console password | console password |
| enable secret | access-group |
| CHAP authentication | service password-encryption |
| VTY password | enable secret |
| service password-encryption | |

## 83. Drag and Drop Question

Routing has been configured on the local router with these commands:
Local(config)# **ip route 0.0.0.0 0.0.0.0 192.168.1.1**
Local(config)# **ip route 10.1.0.0 255.255.255.0 192.168.2.2**
Local(config)# **ip route 10.1.0.0 255.255.0.0 192.168.3.3**
Drag each destination IP address on the left to its correct next hop address on the right.

|  |  |
|---|---|
| 10.1.1.10 | Next hop 192.168.1.1 |
| 10.1.0.14 | |
| 10.2.1.3 | |
| 10.1.4.6 | Next hop 192.168.2.2 |
| 10.1.0.123 | |
| 10.6.8.4 | |
| | Next hop 192.168.3.3 |

Answer:

Routing has been configured on the local router with these commands:
Local(config)# ip route 0.0.0.0 0.0.0.0 192.168.1.1
Local(config)# ip route 10.1.0.0 255.255.255.0 192.168.2.2
Local(config)# ip route 10.1.0.0 255.255.0.0 192.168.3.3
Drag each destination IP address on the left to its correct next hop address on the right.

Left items:
- 10.1.1.10
- 10.1.0.14
- 10.2.1.3
- 10.1.4.6
- 10.1.0.123
- 10.6.8.4

Right items:
- Next hop 192.168.1.1
  - 10.2.1.3
  - 10.6.8.4
- Next hop 192.168.2.2
  - 10.1.0.14
  - 10.1.0.123
- Next hop 192.168.3.3
  - 10.1.1.10
  - 10.1.4.6

## 84. Drag and Drop Question

Drag the cable type on the left to the purpose for which it is best suited on the right. (Not all options are used.)

Left:
- crossover
- null modem
- straight-through
- rollover
- 9-25 pin serial

Right:
- switch access port to router
- switch to switch
- PC COM port to switch

**Answer:**

Drag the cable type on the left to the purpose for which it is best suited on the right. (Not all options are used.)

Left:
- crossover
- null modem
- straight-through
- rollover
- 9-25 pin serial

Right:
- straight-through
- crossover
- rollover

## 85. Drag and Drop Question

Drag each category on the left to its corresponding router output line on the right. Each router output line is the result of a **show ip interface** command. Not all categories are used.

| | |
|---|---|
| Layer 1 problem | Serial0/1 is up, line protocol is up |
| Layer 2 problem | Serial0/1 is up, line protocol is down |
| Layer 3 problem | Serial0/1 is down, line protocol is down |
| port operational | Serial0/1 is administratively down, line protocol is down |
| port disabled | |

Answer:

Drag each category on the left to its corresponding router output line on the right. Each router output line is the result of a **show ip interface** command. Not all categories are used.

| | |
|---|---|
| Layer 1 problem | port operational |
| Layer 2 problem | Layer 2 problem |
| Layer 3 problem | Layer 1 problem |
| port operational | port disabled |
| port disabled | |

## 86. Drag and Drop Question

Drag the Cisco default administrative distance to the appropriate routing protocol or route. (Not all options are used.)

| | |
|---|---|
| 0 | RIP |
| 1 | OSPF |
| 20 | static route referencing IP address of next hop |
| 90 | internal EIGRP route |
| 100 | directly connected network |
| 110 | |
| 120 | |
| 130 | |

Answer:

Drag the Cisco default administrative distance to the appropriate routing protocol or route. (Not all options are used.)

| | |
|---|---|
| 0 | 120 |
| 1 | 110 |
| 20 | 1 |
| 90 | 90 |
| 100 | 0 |
| 110 | |
| 120 | |
| 130 | |

## 87. Drag and Drop Question

Drag the Frame Relay acronym on the left to match its definition on the right. (Not all acronyms are used.)

| | |
|---|---|
| CIR | a router is this type of device |
| DCE | the most common type of virtual circuit |
| DTE | provides status messages between DTE and DCE devices |
| LMI | identifies the virtual connection between the DTE and the switch |
| PVC | |
| SVC | |
| DLCI | |

Answer:

Drag the Frame Relay acronym on the left to match its definition on the right. (Not all acronyms are used.)

| | |
|---|---|
| CIR | DTE |
| DCE | PVC |
| DTE | LMI |
| LMI | DLCI |
| PVC | |
| SVC | |
| DLCI | |

## 88. Drag and Drop Question

A user is unable to connect to the Internet. Based on the layered approach to troubleshooting and beginning with the lowest layer, drag each procedure on the left to its proper category on the right.

| Left | Right |
|---|---|
| verify URL | Step 1 |
| verify NIC operation | Step 2 |
| verify IP configuration | Step 3 |
| verify Ethernet cable connection | Step 4 |

Answer:

A user is unable to connect to the Internet. Based on the layered approach to troubleshooting and beginning with the lowest layer, drag each procedure on the left to its proper category on the right.

| Left | Right |
|---|---|
| verify URL | verify Ethernet cable connection |
| verify NIC operation | verify NIC operation |
| verify IP configuration | verify IP configuration |
| verify Ethernet cable connection | verify URL |

## 89. Drag and Drop Question

Drag each definition on the left to the matching term on the right.

| Left | Right |
|---|---|
| the number of point-to-point links in a transmission path | cost |
| the data capacity of a link | load |
| the amount of time required to move a packet from source to destination | bandwidth |
| the amount of activity on a network resource | hop count |
| usually refers to the bit error rate of each network link | reliability |
| a configurable value based by default on the bandwidth of the interface | delay |

Answer:

Drag each definition on the left to the matching term on the right.

| Left (definitions) | Right (terms) |
|---|---|
| the number of point-to-point links in a transmission path | a configurable value based by default on the bandwidth of the interface |
| the data capacity of a link | the amount of activity on a network resource |
| the amount of time required to move a packet from source to destination | the data capacity of a link |
| the amount of activity on a network resource | the number of point-to-point links in a transmission path |
| usually refers to the bit error rate of each network link | usually refers to the bit error rate of each network link |
| a configurable value based by default on the bandwidth of the interface | the amount of time required to move a packet from source to destination |

## 90. Drag and Drop Question

Match the terms on the left with the appropriate OSI layer on the right. (Not all options are used.)

Left:
- frames
- packets
- UDP
- IP addresses
- segments
- MAC addresses
- windowing
- routing

Right:
- Network Layer
- Transport Layer

Answer:

| | |
|---|---|
| frames | **Network Layer** |
| packets | packets |
| UDP | IP addresses |
| IP addresses | routing |
| segments | **Transport Layer** |
| MAC addresses | UDP |
| windowing | segments |
| routing | windowing |

**91. Lab Simulation Question - ACL-1**

*A network associate is adding security to the configuration of the Corp1 router. The user on host C*
*should be able to use a web browser to access financial information from the Finance Web Server.*
*No other hosts from the LAN nor the Core should be able to use a web browser to access this*
*server. Since there are multiple resources for the corporation at this location including other*
*resources on the Finance Web Server, all other traffic should be allowed.*
*The task is to create and apply an access-list with no more than three statements that will allow*
*ONLY host C web access to the Finance Web Server. No other hosts will have web access to the*
*Finance Web Server. All other traffic is permitted.*
*Access to the router CLI can be gained by clicking on the appropriate host.*
*All passwords have been temporarily set to "cisco".*
*The Core connection uses an IP address of 198.18.196.65*
*The computers in the Hosts LAN have been assigned addresses of 192.168.33.1 - 192.168.33.254*
*Host A 192.168.33.1*
*Host B 192.168.33.2*
*Host C 192.168.33.3*
*Host D 192.168.33.4*
*The servers in the Server LAN have been assigned addresses of 172.22.242.17 - 172.22.242.30*
*The Finance Web Server is assigned an IP address of 172.22.242.23.*

A network associate is adding security to the configuration of the Corp1 router. The user on host C should be able to use a web browser to access financial information from the Finance Web Server. No other hosts from the LAN nor the Core should be able to use a web browser to access this server. Since there are multiple resources for the corporation at this location including other resources on the Finance Web Server, all other traffic should be allowed.

The task is to create and apply an access-list with no more than three statements that will allow ONLY host C web access to the Finance Web Server. No other hosts will have web access to the Finance Web Server. All other traffic is permitted.
Access to the router CLI can be gained by clicking on the appropriate host.

All passwords have been temporarily set to "cisco".
The Core connection uses an IP address of 198.18.196.65
The computers in the Hosts LAN have been assigned addresses of 192.168.33.1 - 192.168.33.254.
- host A 192.168.33.1
- host B 192.168.33.2
- host C 192.168.33.3
- host D 192.168.33.4

The servers in the Server LAN have been assigned addresses of 172.22.242.17 - 172.22.242.30
The Finance Web Server is assigned an IP address of 172.22.242.23

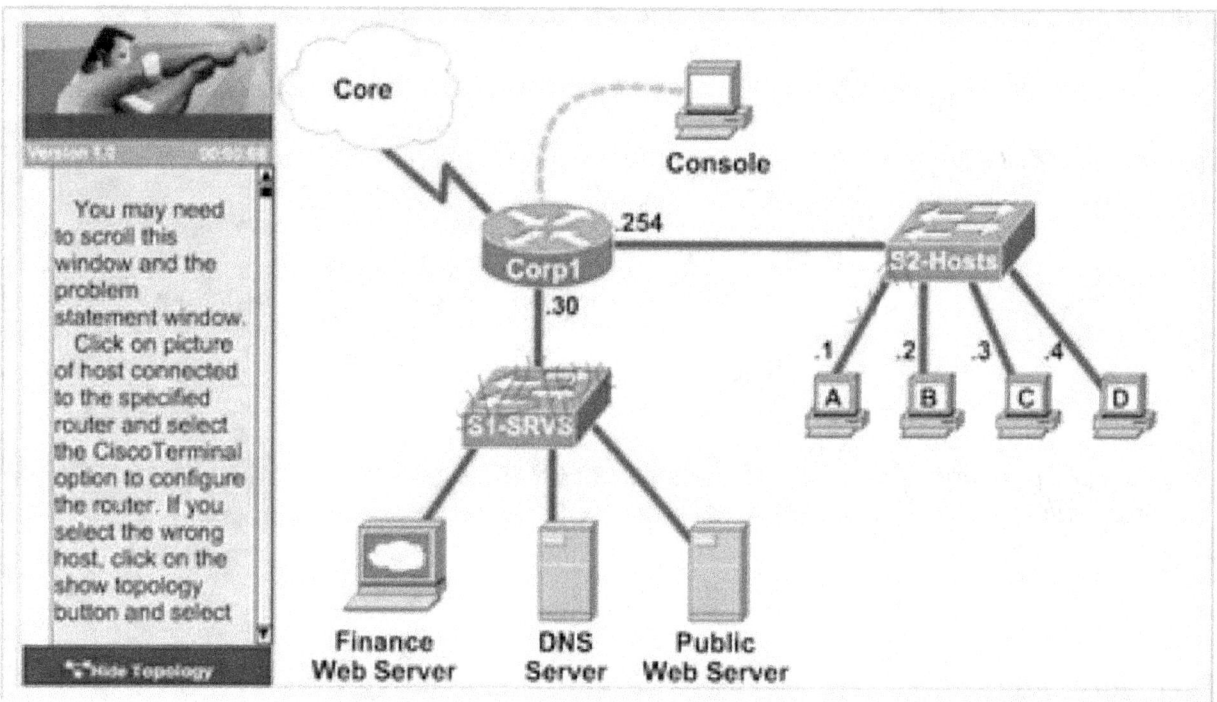

Answer:
Corp1>enable
Password: cisco
We should create an access-list and apply it to the interface which is connected to the Servers LAN
interface, because it can filter out traffic from both Sw-Hosts and Core networks. The Server LAN
network has been assigned addresses of 172.22.242.17 – 172.22.242.30 so we can guess the

interface connected to them has an IP address of 172.22.242.30 (.30 is the number shown in the
figure). Use the "show ip interface brief" command to check which interface has the IP address of
172.22.242.30.

Corp1#show ip interface brief
Interface IP-Address OK? Method Status Protocol
FastEthernet0/0 192.168.33.254 YES manual up up
FastEthernet0/1 172.22.242.30 YES manual up up
Serial0/0 198.18.196.65 YES manual up up

We learn that interface FastEthernet0/1 is the interface connected to Server LAN network. It is the
interface we will apply our access-list (for outbound direction).
Corp1#configure terminal
Our access-list needs to allow host C – 192.168.33.3 to the Finance Web Server 172.22.242.23
via web (port 80)
Corp1(config)#access-list 100 permit tcp host 192.168.33.3 host 172.22.242.23 eq 80
Deny other hosts access to the Finance Web Server via web
Corp1(config)#access-list 100 deny tcp any host 172.22.242.23 eq 80
All other traffic is permitted
Corp1(config)#access-list 100 permit ip any any
Apply this access-list to Fa0/1 interface (outbound direction)
Corp1(config)#interface fa0/1
Corp1(config-if)#ip access-group 100 out
Notice: We have to apply the access-list to Fa0/1 interface (not Fa0/0 interface) so that the access-
list can filter traffic coming from both the LAN and the Core networks. If we apply access list to the
inbound interface we can only filter traffic from the LAN network.

In the real exam, just click on host C and open its web browser. In the address box type
http://172.22.242.23 to check if you are allowed to access Finance Web Server or not. If your
configuration is correct then you can access it.
Click on other hosts (A, B and D) and check to make sure you can't access Finance Web Server
from these hosts.
Finally, save the configuration
Corp1(config-if)#end
Corp1#copy running-config startup-config
This configuration only prevents hosts from accessing Finance Web Server via web but if this server
supports other traffic – like FTP, SMTP... then other hosts can access it, too.
Notice: In the real exam, you might be asked to allow other host (A, B or D) to access the Finance

Web Server so please read the requirement carefully.

**Modification #1**

A network associate is adding security to the configuration of the Corp router. The user on host B
should be able to access the Finance Web Server. Host B should be denied to access other server
on S1-SRVS network. Since there are multiple resources for the corporation at this location
including other resources on the Finance Web Server, all other traffic should be allowed.
The task is to create and apply a numbered access-list with no more than three statements that will
allow ONLY host B access to the Finance Web Server. Deny host B from accessing the other
servers. All other traffic is permitted.

access-list 100 permit ip host 192.168.33.2 host 172.22.242.23
access-list 100 deny ip host 192.168.33.2 172.22.242.16 0.0.0.15
access-list 100 permit ip any any

**Modification #2**

A network associate is adding security to the configuration of the Corp1 router. The user on host C
should be able to access the Finance Web Server. No other hosts from the LAN nor the Core
should be able access this server. All other traffic should be allowed.
The task is to create and apply a numbered access-list with no more than three statements that will
allow ONLY host C access the Finance Web Server. No other hosts will have access to the Finance
Web Server. All other traffic is permitted.

access-list 100 permit ip host 192.168.33.3 host 172.22.242.23
access-list 100 deny ip any host 172.22.242.23
access-list 100 permit ip any any

**Modification #3**

A network associate is adding security to the configuration of the Corp1 router. The user on host C
should be able to use a web browser to access financial information from the Finance Web Server.
Other access from host C to Finance Web Server should be denied. No other hosts from the LAN
nor the Core should be able to access the Finance Web Server. All other traffic should be allowed.
The task is to create and apply a numbered access-list with no more than three statements that will
allow ONLY host C web access to the Finance Web Server. Also host C should be denied to access
any other services of Finance Web Server. No other hosts will access to the Finance Web Server.
All other traffic is permitted.

access-list 100 permit tcp host 192.168.33.3 host 172.22.242.23 eq 80
access-list 100 deny ip any host 172.22.242.23
access-list 100 permit ip any any

Modification #4
A network associate is adding security to the configuration of the Corp1 router. The user on host D
should be able to use a web browser to access financial information from the Finance Web Server.
Other access from host C to Finance Web Server should be denied. No other hosts from the LAN
nor the Core should be able to access the Finance Web Server. All hosts from the LAN nor the
Core should able to access public web server.
The task is to create and apply a numbered access-list with no more than three statements that will
allow ONLY host D should be able to use a web browser(HTTP)to access the Finance Web Server.
Other types of access from host D to the Finance Web Server should be blocked. All access from hosts in the Core or local LAN to the Finance Web Server should be blocked. All hosts in the Core
and local LAN should be able to access the Public Web Server.
access-list 100 permit tcp host 192.168.33.3 host 172.22.242.23 eq 80
access-list 100 deny ip any host 172.22.242.23
access-list 100 permit ip any any

## 92. Drag and Drop Question

Refer to the exhibit. PC_1 is exchanging packets with the FTP server. Consider the packets as they leave RouterB interface Fa0/1 towards RouterA. Drag the correct frame and packet addresses to their place in the table.

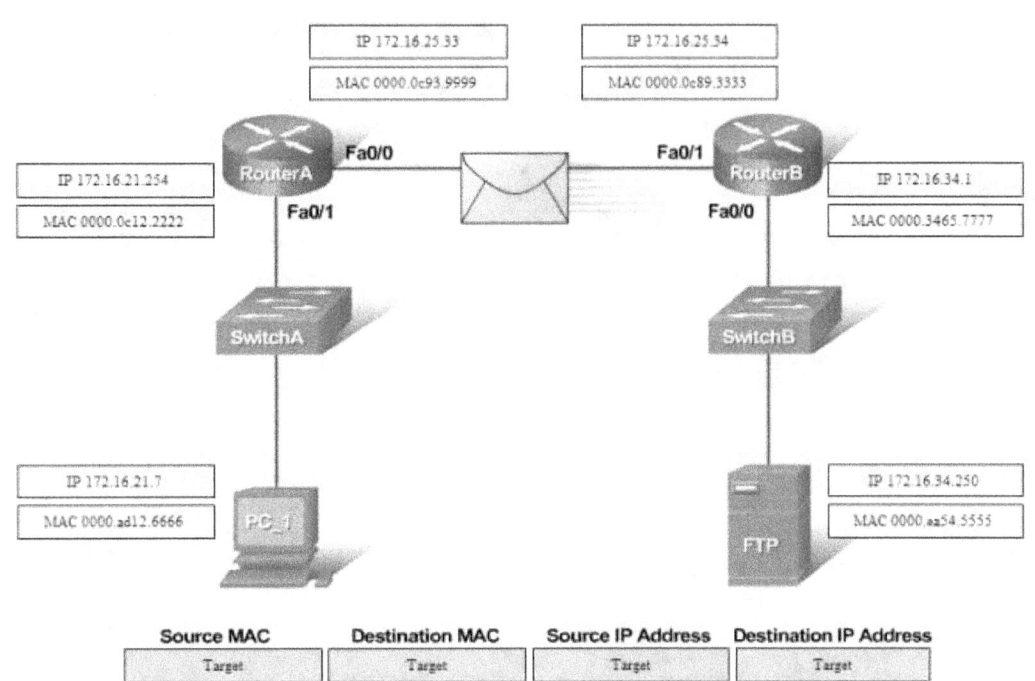

**Answer:**

Answer:

Refer to the exhibit. PC_1 is exchanging packets with the FTP server. Consider the packets as they leave RouterB interface Fa0/1 towards RouterA. Drag the correct frame and packet addresses to their place in the table.

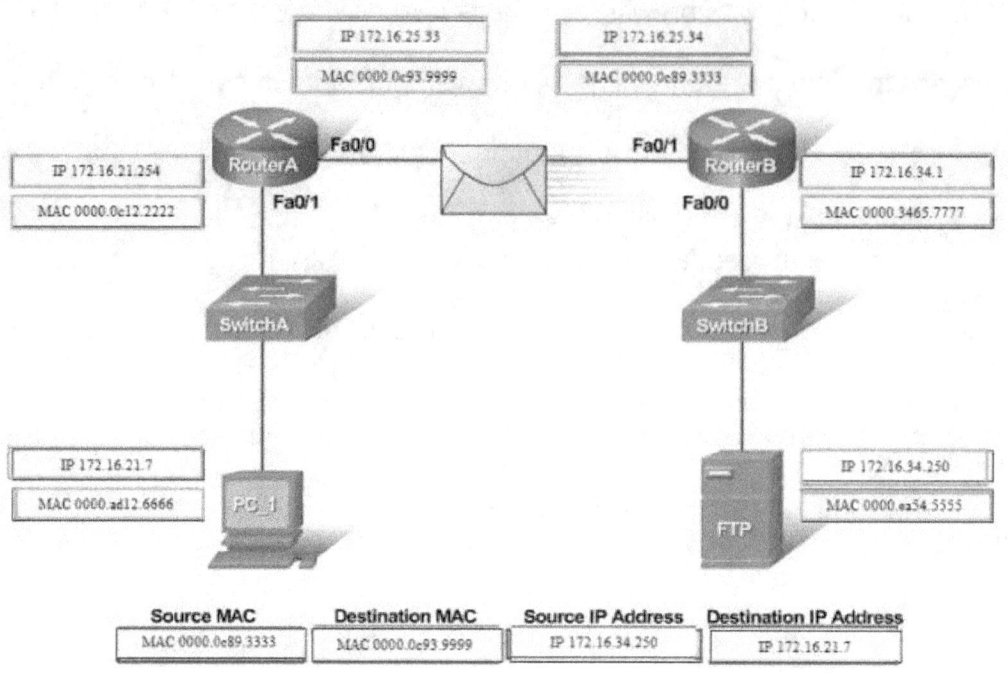

| Source MAC | Destination MAC | Source IP Address | Destination IP Address |
|---|---|---|---|
| MAC 0000.0e89.3333 | MAC 0000.0e93.9999 | IP 172.16.34.250 | IP 172.16.21.7 |

## 93. Drag and Drop Question

Refer to the exhibit. PC_1 is sending packets to the FTP server. Consider the packets as they leave RouterA interface Fa0/0 towards RouterB. Drag the correct frame and packet address to their place in the table.

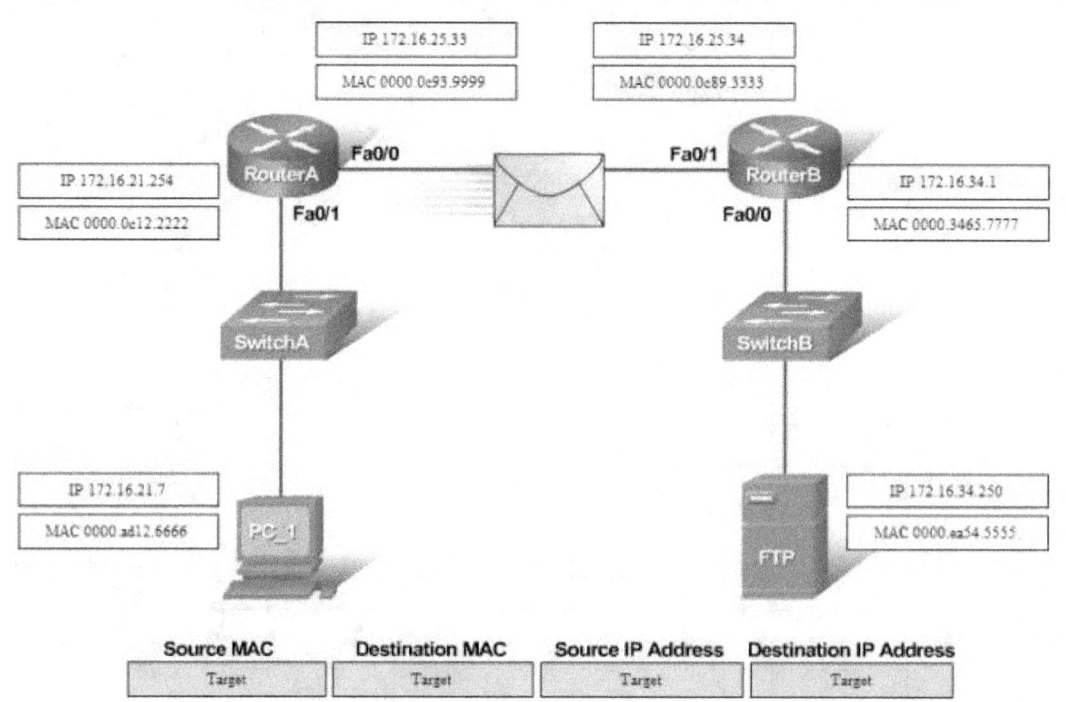

| Source MAC | Destination MAC | Source IP Address | Destination IP Address |
|---|---|---|---|
| Target | Target | Target | Target |

**Answer:**

Refer to the exhibit. PC_1 is sending packets to the FTP server. Consider the packets as they leave RouterA interface Fa0/0 towards RouterB. Drag the correct frame and packet address to their place in the table.

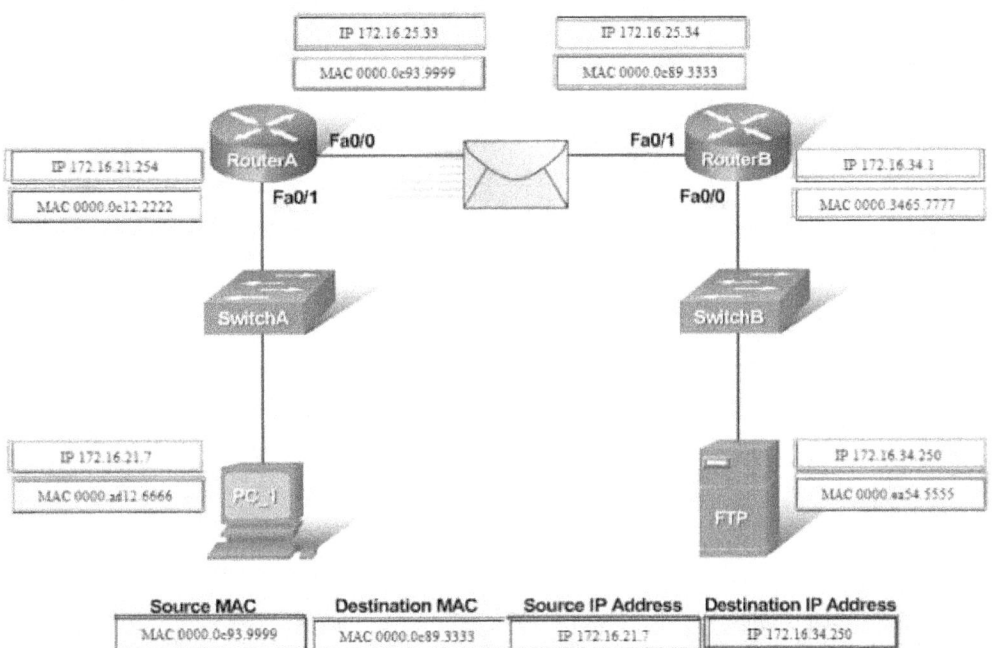

## 94. Drag and Drop Question

Refer to the exhibit. Complete this network diagram by dragging the correct device name or description to the correct location. Not all the names or descriptions will be used.

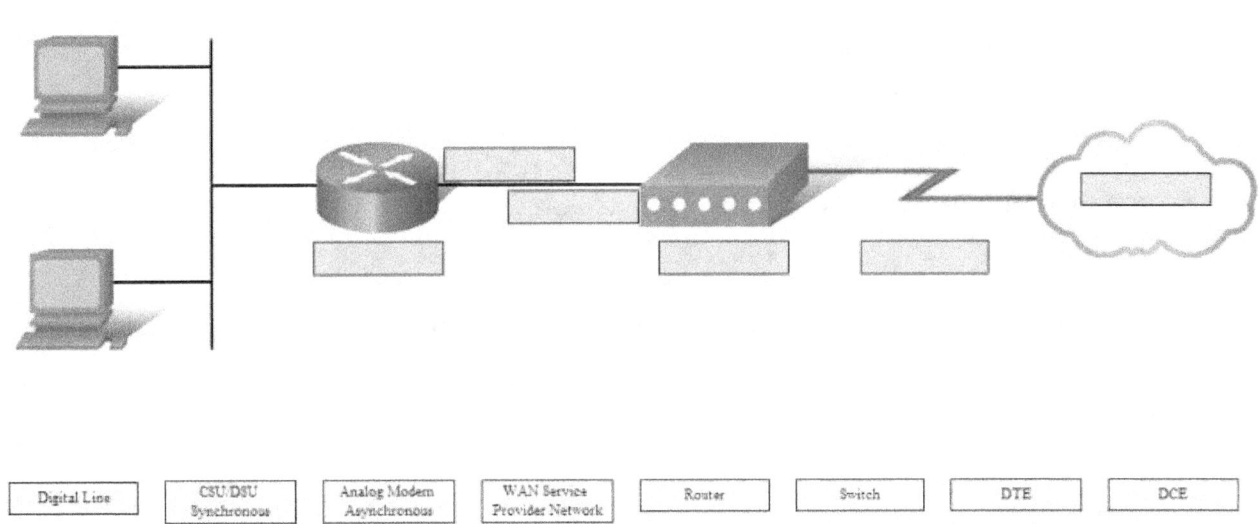

**Answer:**

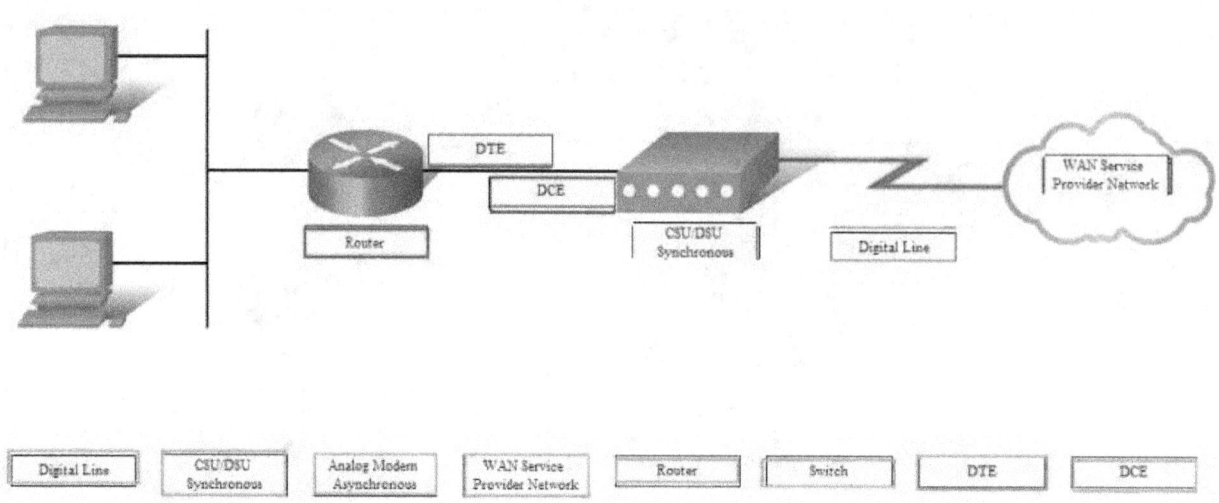

Refer to the exhibit. Complete this network diagram by dragging the correct device name or description to the correct location. Not all the names or descriptions will be used.

### 95. Hotspot Question

**Instructions**

An administrator is trying to ping and telnet from SwitchC to RouterC with the results shown below.

```
SwitchC>
SwitchC> ping 10.4.4.3
Type escape sequence to abort.
Sending 5, 100-byte ICMP Echos to 10.4.4.3, timeout is 2 seconds:
U.U.U
Success rate is 0 percent (0/5)
SwitchC>
SwitchC> telnet 10.4.4.3
Trying 10.4.4.3 ...
% Destination unreachable; gateway or host down
SwitchC>
```

Click the console connected to RouterC and issue the appropriate commands to answer the questions.

**Topology**

## Topology

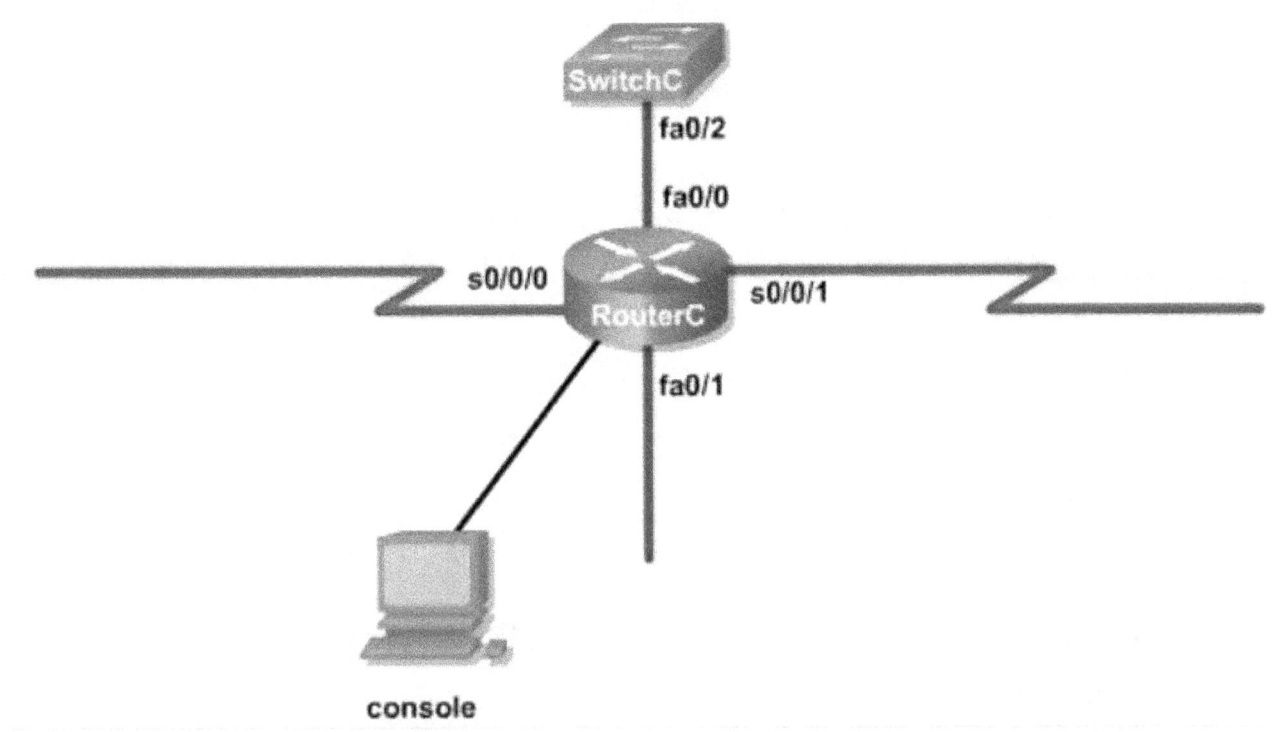

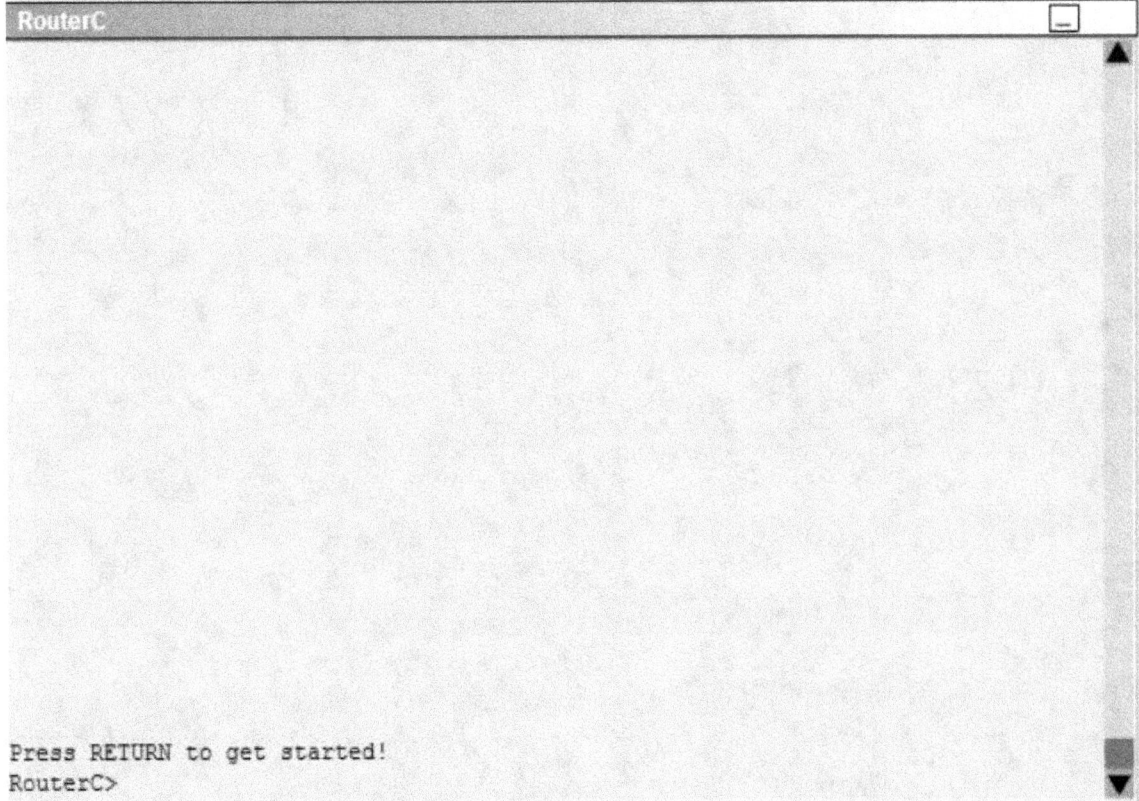

```
<output omitted>

interface Loopback1
 ip address 172.16.4.1.255.255.255.0
!
interface Loopback2
 ip address 10.145.145.1  255.255.255.0
 ipv6 address 2001:410:2:3::/64 eui-64
!
interface FastEthernet0/0
 ip address 10.4.4.3.255.255.255.0
 ip access-group 106 in
 duplex auto
 speed auto
!
interface FastEthernet0/1
 no ip address
 shutdown
 duplex auto
speed auto
!
```

```
interface Serial0/0/0
 bandwidth 64
 no ip address
 ip access-group 102 out
 encapsulation frame-relay
 ip ospf authentication
 ip ospf authentication
 ip ospf authentication-key san-fran
!
interface Serial0/0/0.1 point-to-point
 ip address 10.140.3.2 255.255.255.0
 ip authentication mode eigrp 100 md5
 ip authentication key-chain eigrp 100 icndchain
 frame-relay interface-dlci 120
!
interface Serail0/0/1
 bandwidth 64
 ip address 10.45.45.1 255.255.255.0
 ip access-group 102 in
 ip authentication mode eigrp 100 md5
 ip authentication key-chain eigrp 100 icndchain
 ip ospf authentication
 ip ospf authentication-key san-fran
 ipv6 address 2001:410:2:10::/64 eui-64
!
```

```
router eigrp 100
 network 10.0.0.0
 network 172.16.0.0
 network 192.168.2.0
 not auto-summary
!
router ospf 100
 log-adjacency-changes
 network 10.4.4.3 0.0.0.0 area 0
 network 10.45.45.1 0.0.0.0 area 0
 network 10.140.3.2 0.0.0.0 area 0
 network 192.168.2.62 0.0.0.0 area 0
!
router rip
 version 2
 network 10.0.0.0
 network 172.16.0.0
!
ip default-gateway 10.1.1.2
!
!
ip http server
no ip http secure-server
!
```

```
access-list 102 permit tcp any any eq ftp
access-list 102 permit tcp any any eq ftp-data
access-list 102 deny tcp any any eq telnet
access-list 102 deny icmp any any echo-reply
access-list 102 permit ip any any

access-list 104 permit tcp any any eq ftp
access-list 104 permit tcp any any eq ftp-data
access-list 104 deny tcp any any eq telnet
access-list 104 permit icmp any any echo
access-list 104 deny icmp any any echo-reply
access-list 104 permit ip any any

access-list 106 permit tcp any any eq ftp
access-list 106 permit tcp any any ftp-data
access-list 106 deny tcp any any eq telnet
access-list 106 permit icmp any any echo-reply
access-list 110 permit udp any any eq domain
access-list 110 permit udp any eq domain any
access-list 110 permit tcp any any eq domain
access-list 110 permit tcp any eq domain any
access-list 110 permit tcp any any

access-list 114 permit ip 10.4.4.0.0.0.0.255 any

access-list 115 permit ip 0.0.0.0 255.255.255.0 any

access-list 122 deny tcp any any
access-list 122 deny imp any any echo-reply
access-list 122 permit ip any any
!
<output omitted>
```

**Which will fix the issue and allow ONLY ping to work while keeping telnet disabled?**

A. Correctly assign an IP address to interface fa0/1.
B. Change the ip access-group command on fa0/0 from "in* to "our.
C. Remove access-group 106 in from interface fa0/0 and add access-group 115 in.
D. Remove access-group 102 out from interface s0/0/0 and add access-group 114 in
E. Remove access-group 106 in from interface fa0/0 and add access-group 104 in.

**Answer: E**
**Explanation:**
Let's have a look at the access list 104:

```
access-list 104 permit tcp any any eq ftp
access-list 104 permit tcp any any eq ftp-data
access-list 104 deny tcp any any eq telent
access-list 104 permit icmp any any echo
access-list 104 permit icmp any any echo-reply
access-list 104 permit ip any any
```

The question does not ask about ftp traffic so we don't care about the two first lines. The 3rd line denies all telnet traffic and the 4th line allows icmp traffic to be sent (ping). Remember that the access list 104 is applied on the inbound direction so the 5th line "access-list 104 deny icmp any any echo-reply" will not affect our icmp traffic because the "echo-reply" message will be sent over the outbound direction.

**96. Hotspot Question**

**Instructions**

An administrator is trying to ping and telnet from SwitchC to RouterC with the results shown below.

```
SwitchC>
SwitchC> ping 10.4.4.3
Type escape sequence to abort.
Sending 5, 100-byte ICMP Echos to 10.4.4.3, timeout is 2 seconds:
U.U.U
Success rate is 0 percent (0/5)
SwitchC>
SwitchC> telnet 10.4.4.3
Trying 10.4.4.3 ...
% Destination unreachable; gateway or host down
SwitchC>
```

Click the console connected to RouterC and issue the appropriate commands to answer the questions.

**Topology**

## Topology

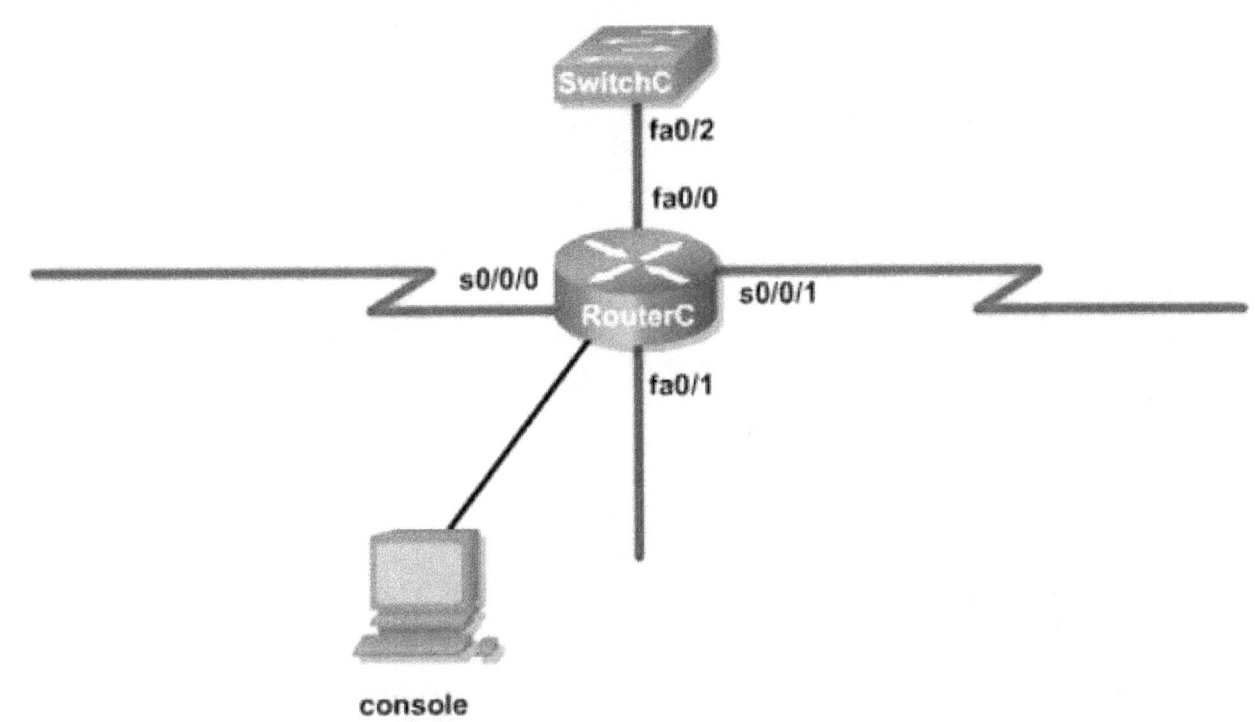

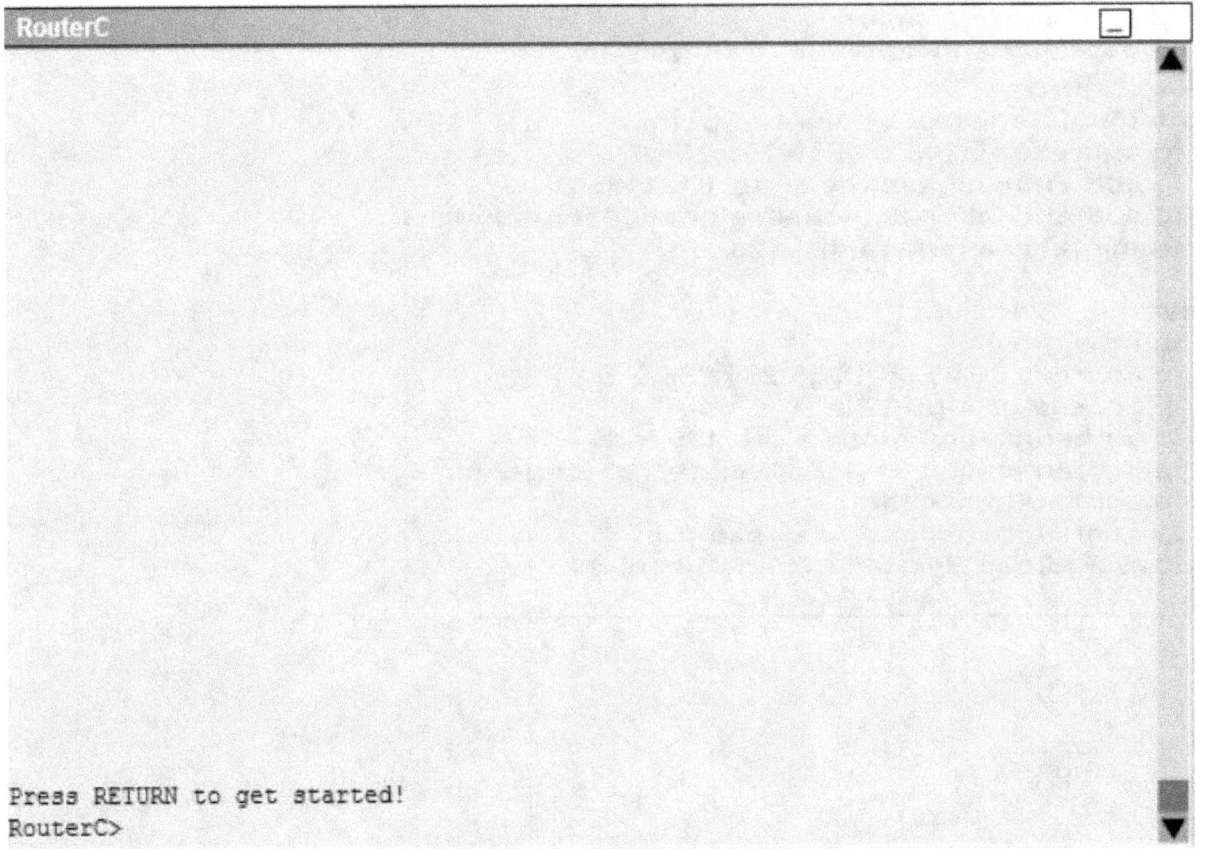

```
<output omitted>

interface Loopback1
 ip address 172.16.4.1 255.255.255.0
!
interface Loopback2
 ip address 10.145.145.1  255.255.255.0
 ipv6 address 2001:410:2:3::/64 eui-64
!
interface FastEthernet0/0
 ip address 10.4.4.3 255.255.255.0
 ip access-group 106 in
 duplex auto
 speed auto
!
interface FastEthernet0/1
 no ip address
 shutdown
 duplex auto
 speed auto
!
interface Serial0/0/0
 bandwidth 64
 no ip address
 ip access-group 102 out
 encapsulation frame-relay
 ip ospf authentication
 ip ospf authentication
 ip ospf authentication-key san-fran
!
interface Serial0/0/0.1 point-to-point
 ip address 10.140.3.2 255.255.255.0
 ip authentication mode eigrp 100 md5
 ip authentication key-chain eigrp 100 icndchain
 frame-relay interface-dlci 120
!
interface Serial0/0/1
 bandwidth 64
 ip address 10.45.45.1 255.255.255.0
 ip access-group 102 in
 ip authentication mode eigrp 100 md5
 ip authentication key-chain eigrp 100 icndchain
 ip ospf authentication
 ip ospf authentication-key san-fran
 ipv6 address 2001:410:2:10::/64 eui-64
!
```

```
router eigrp 100
 network 10.0.0.0
 network 172.16.0.0
 network 192.168.2.0
 not auto-summary
!
router ospf 100
 log-adjacency-changes
 network 10.4.4.3 0.0.0.0 area 0
 network 10.45.45.1 0.0.0.0 area 0
 network 10.140.3.2 0.0.0.0 area 0
 network 192.168.2.62 0.0.0.0 area 0
!
router rip
 version 2
 network 10.0.0.0
 network 172.16.0.0
!
ip default-gateway 10.1.1.2
!
!
ip http server
no ip http secure-server
!
```

```
access-list 102 permit tcp any any eq ftp
access-list 102 permit tcp any any eq ftp-data
access-list 102 deny tcp any any eq telnet
access-list 102 deny icmp any any echo-reply
access-list 102 permit ip any any

access-list 104 permit tcp any any eq ftp
access-list 104 permit tcp any any eq ftp-data
access-list 104 deny tcp any any eq telnet
access-list 104 permit icmp any any echo
access-list 104 deny icmp any any echo-reply
access-list 104 permit ip any any

access-list 106 permit tcp any any eq ftp
access-list 106 permit tcp any any ftp-data
access-list 106 deny tcp any any eq telnet
access-list 106 permit icmp any any echo-reply
access-list 110 permit udp any any eq domain
access-list 110 permit udp any eq domain any
access-list 110 permit tcp any any eq domain
access-list 110 permit tcp any eq domain any
access-list 110 permit tcp any any

access-list 114 permit ip 10.4.4.0.0.0.0.255 any

access-list 115 permit ip 0.0.0.0 255.255.255.0 any

access-list 122 deny tcp any any
access-list 122 deny imp any any echo-reply
access-list 122 permit ip any any
!
<output omitted>
```

What would be the effect of issuing the command ip access-group 114 in to the fa0/0 interface?

A. Attempts to telnet to the router would fail.
B. It would allow all traffic from the 10.4.4.0 network.
C. IP traffic would be passed through the interface but TCP and UDP traffic would not.
D. Routing protocol updates for the 10.4.4.0 network would not be accepted from the fa0/0 interface.

Answer: B
Explanation:
From the output of access-list 114: access-list 114 permit ip 10.4.4.0 0.0.0.255 any we can easily understand that this access list allows all traffic (ip) from 10.4.4.0/24 network.

97. Hotspot Question

## Instructions

An administrator is trying to ping and telnet from SwitchC to RouterC with the results shown below.

SwitchC>
SwitchC> ping 10.4.4.3
Type escape sequence to abort.
Sending 5, 100-byte ICMP Echos to 10.4.4.3, timeout is 2 seconds:
U.U.U
Success rate is 0 percent (0/5)
SwitchC>
SwitchC> telnet 10.4.4.3
Trying 10.4.4.3 ...
% Destination unreachable; gateway or host down
SwitchC>

Click the console connected to RouterC and issue the appropriate commands to answer the questions.

## Topology

## Topology

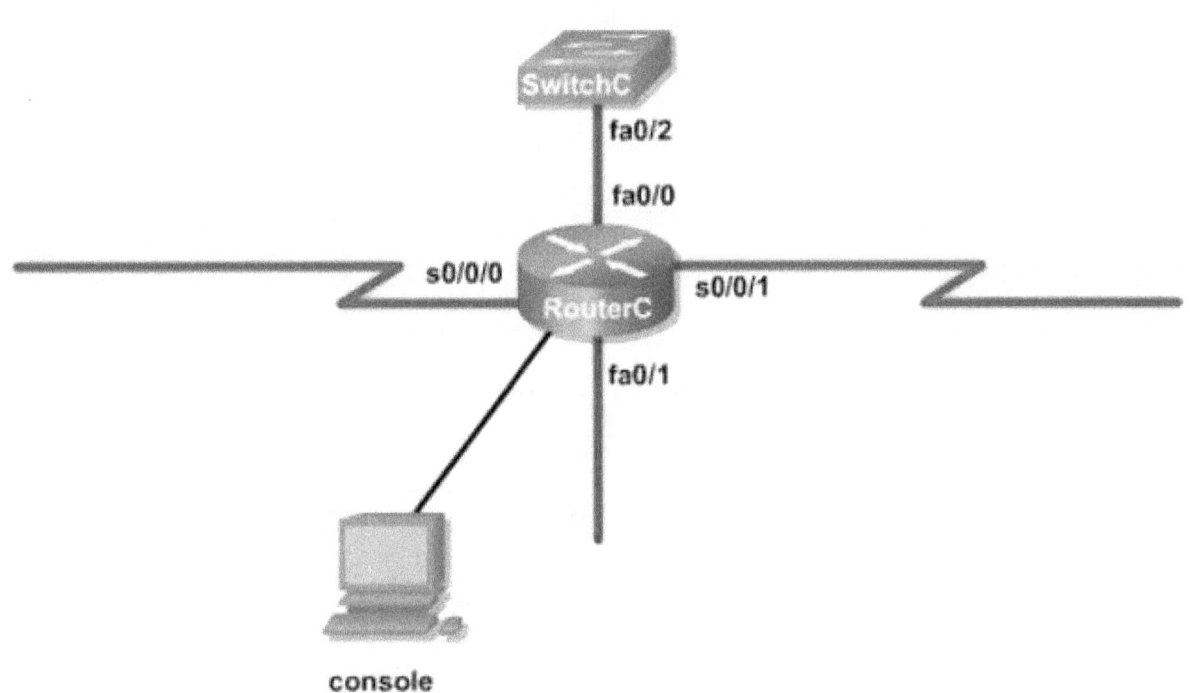

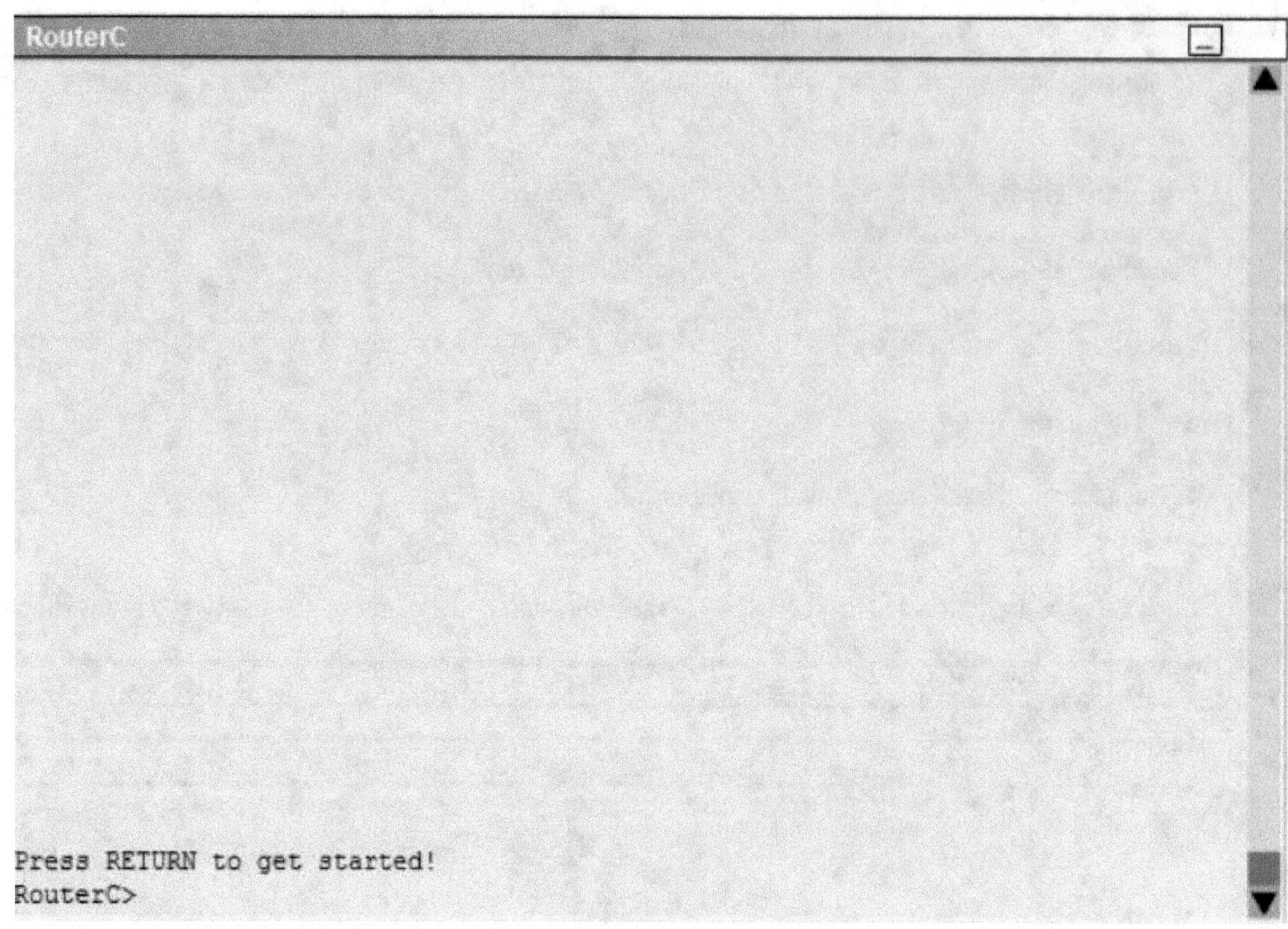

```
<output omitted>

interface Loopback1
  ip address 172.16.4.1 255.255.255.0
!
interface Loopback2
  ip address 10.145.145.1  255.255.255.0
  ipv6 address 2001:410:2:3::/64 eui-64
!
interface FastEthernet0/0
  ip address 10.4.4.3 255.255.255.0
  ip access-group 106 in
  duplex auto
  speed auto
!
interface FastEthernet0/1
  no ip address
  shutdown
  duplex auto
 speed auto
!
interface Serial0/0/0
  bandwidth 64
  no ip address
  ip access-group 102 out
  encapsulation frame-relay
  ip ospf authentication
  ip ospf authentication
  ip ospf authentication-key san-fran
!
interface Serial0/0/0.1 point-to-point
  ip address 10.140.3.2 255.255.255.0
  ip authentication mode eigrp 100 md5
  ip authentication key-chain eigrp 100 icndchain
  frame-relay interface-dlci 120
!
interface Serail0/0/1
  bandwidth 64
  ip address 10.45.45.1 255.255.255.0
  ip access-group 102 in
  ip authentication mode eigrp 100 md5
  ip authentication key-chain eigrp 100 icndchain
  ip ospf authentication
  ip ospf authentication-key san-fran
  ipv6 address 2001:410:2:10::/64 eui-64
!
```

```
router eigrp 100
  network 10.0.0.0
  network 172.16.0.0
  network 192.168.2.0
  not auto-summary
!
router ospf 100
  log-adjacency-changes
  network 10.4.4.3 0.0.0.0 area 0
  network 10.45.45.1 0.0.0.0 area 0
  network 10.140.3.2 0.0.0.0 area 0
  network 192.168.2.62 0.0.0.0 area 0
!
router rip
  version 2
  network 10.0.0.0
  network 172.16.0.0
!
ip default-gateway 10.1.1.2
!
!
ip http server
no ip http secure-server
!
```

```
access-list 102 permit tcp any any eq ftp
access-list 102 permit tcp any any eq ftp-data
access-list 102 deny tcp any any eq telnet
access-list 102 deny icmp any any echo-reply
access-list 102 permit ip any any

access-list 104 permit tcp any any eq ftp
access-list 104 permit tcp any any eq ftp-data
access-list 104 deny tcp any any eq telnet
access-list 104 permit icmp any any echo
access-list 104 deny icmp any any echo-reply
access-list 104 permit ip any any

access-list 106 permit tcp any any eq ftp
access-list 106 permit tcp any any ftp-data
access-list 106 deny tcp any any eq telnet
access-list 106 permit icmp any any echo-reply
access-list 110 permit udp any any eq domain
access-list 110 permit udp any eq domain any
access-list 110 permit tcp any any eq domain
access-list 110 permit tcp any eq domain any
access-list 110 permit tcp any any

access-list 114 permit ip 10.4.4.0.0.0.0.255 any

access-list 115 permit ip 0.0.0.0 255.255.255.0 any

access-list 122 deny tcp any any
access-list 122 deny imp any any echo-reply
access-list 122 permit ip any any
!
<output omitted>
```

What would be the effect of Issuing the command ip access-group 115 in on the s0/0/1 interface?
A. No host could connect to RouterC through s0/0/1.
B. Telnet and ping would work but routing updates would fail.
C. FTP, FTP-DATA, echo, and www would work but telnet would fail.
D. Only traffic from the 10.4.4.0 network would pass through the interface.

Answer: A
Explanation:
First let's see what was configured on interface S0/0/1:

```
interface Serial0/0/1
 bandwidth 64
 ip address 10.45.45.1 255.255.255.0
 ip access-group 102 in
```

98. Refer to the exhibit. Based on the information given, which switch will be elected root bridge and why?

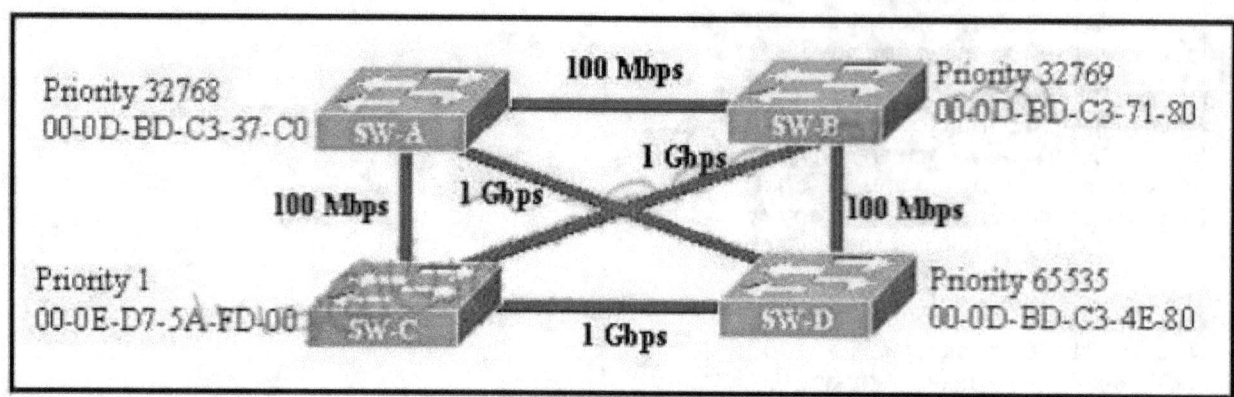

A. Switch A, because it has the lowest MAC address
B. Switch A, because it is the most centrally located switch
C. Switch B, because it has the highest MAC address
D. Switch C, because it is the most centrally located switch
E. Switch C, because it has the lowest priority
F. Switch D, because it has the highest priority

Answer: E

99. Lab Simulation Question - EIGRP

CCNA.com has a small network that is using EIGRP as its IGP. All routers should be running an EIGRP AS number of 12. Router MGT is also running static routing to the ISP.

CCNA.com has recently adding the ENG router. Currently, the ENG router does not have connectivity to the ISP router. All other interconnectivity and Internet access for the existing locations of the company are working properly.

**The task** is to identify the fault(s) and correct the router configuration(s) to provide full connectivity between the routers.

**Access to the router CLI can be gained by clicking on the appropriate host.**
All passwords on all routers are **cisco**.
IP addresses are listed in the chart below.

MGT
Fa0/0 - 192.168.77.33
S1/0 - 198.0.18.6
S0/0 - 192.168.27.9
S0/1 - 192.168.50.21

ENG
Fa0/0 - 192.168.77.34
Fa1/0 - 192.168.12.17
Fa0/1 - 192.168.12.1

Parts1
Fa0/0 - 192.168.12.33
Fa0/1 - 192.168.12.49
S0/0 - 192.168.27.10

Parts2
Fa0/0 - 192.168.12.65
Fa0/1 - 192.168.12.81
S0/1 - 192.168.50.22

- You may need to scroll this window and the problem statement window.
- Click on picture of host connected to the specified router and select the CiscoTerminal option to configure the router. If you select the wrong host, click on the show topology

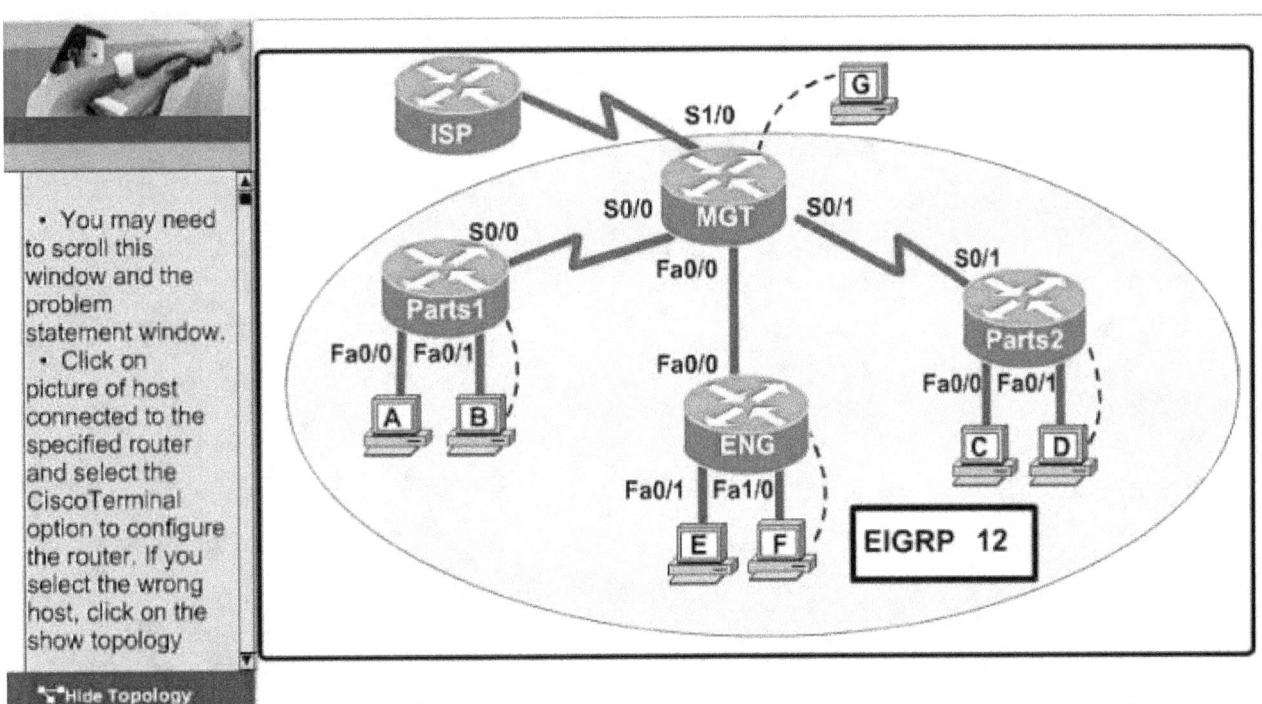

**Answer:**
First we should check the configuration of the ENG Router.
Click the console PC "F" and enter the following commands.
ENG> enable
Password: cisco
ENG# show running-config
Building configuration...
Current configuration : 770 bytes
!
version 12.2
no service timestamps log datetime msec
no service timestamps debug datetime msec
no service password-encryption
!
hostname ENG
!
enable secret 5 $1$mERr$hx5rVt7rPNoS4wqbXKX7m0
!
interface FastEthernet0/0
ip address 192.168.77.34 255.255.255.252
duplex auto
speed auto
!
interface FastEthernet0/1
ip address 192.168.60.65 255.255.255.240
duplex auto
speed auto
!
interface FastEthernet1/0
ip address 192.168.60.81 255.255.255.240
duplex auto
speed auto
!
router eigrp 22
network 192.168.77.0
network 192.168.60.0
no auto-summary
!
ip classless
!
line con 0
line vty 0 4
login
!
end
ENG#
From the output above, we know that this router was wrongly configured with an autonomous
number (AS) of 22. When the AS numbers among routers are mismatched, no adjacency is

formed.
(You should check the AS numbers on other routers for sure)
To solve this problem, we simply re-configure router ENG router with the following commands:
ENG# conf t
ENG(config)# no router eigrp 22
ENG(config)# router eigrp 12
ENG(config-router)# network 192.168.60.0
ENG(config-router)# network 192.168.77.0
ENG(config-router)# no auto-summary
ENG(config-router)# end
ENG# copy running-config startup-config
Second we should check the configuration of the MGT Router.
Click the console PC "G" and enter the following commands.
MGT> enable
Password: cisco
MGT# show running-config
Building configuration...
Current configuration : 1029 bytes
!
version 12.2
no service timestamps log datetime msec
no service timestamps debug datetime msec
no service password-encryption
!
hostname MGT
!
enable secret 5 $1$mERr$hx5rVt7rPNoS4wqbXKX7m0
!
interface FastEthernet0/0
ip address 192.168.77.33 255.255.255.252
duplex auto
speed auto
!
interface Serial0/0
ip address 192.168.36.13 255.255.255.252
clock rate 64000
!
interface Serial0/1
ip address 192.168.60.25 255.255.255.252
clock rate 64000
!
interface Serial1/0
ip address 198.0.18.6 255.255.255.252
!
interface Serial1/1
no ip address
shutdown
!

```
interface Serial1/2
no ip address
shutdown
!
interface Serial1/3
no ip address
shutdown
!
router eigrp 12
network 192.168.36.0
network 192.168.60.0
network 192.168.85.0
network 198.0.18.0
no auto-summary
!
ip classless
ip route 0.0.0.0 0.0.0.0 198.0.18.5
!
line con 0
line vty 0 4
login
!
end
MGT#
```

Notice that it is missing a definition to the network ENG. Therefore we have to add it so that it can
recognize ENG router

```
MGT# conf t
MGT(config)# router eigrp 12
MGT(config-router)# network 192.168.77.0
MGT(config-router)# end
MGT# copy running-config startup-config
```

Now the whole network will work well. You should check again with ping command from router
ENG to other routers!

In Short:
ENG Router
```
ENG>enable
Password: cisco ENG# conf t
ENG(config)# no router eigrp 22
ENG(config)# router eigrp 12
ENG(config-router)# network 192.168.60.0
ENG(config-router)# network 192.168.77.0
ENG(config-router)# no auto-summary
ENG(config-router)# end
ENG# copy running-config startup-config
```
MGT Router
```
MGT>enable
Password: cisco MGT# conf t
```

```
MGT(config)# router eigrp 12
MGT(config-router)# network 192.168.77.0
MGT(config-router)# end
MGT# copy running-config startup-config
```
Some Modification in Question
After adding ENG router, no routing updates are being exchanged between MGT and the new
location. All other inter connectivity for the existing locations of the company are working properly.
But Internet connection for existing location including Remote1 and Remote2 networks are not
working.

Faults Identified:
1. Incorrect Autonomous System Number configured in ENG router.
2. MGT router does not advertise route to the new router ENG.
3. Internet Connection is not working all stations.

We need to correct the above two configuration mistakes to have full connectivity

Steps:
1. ENG Router: Change the Autonomous System Number of ENG
2. Perimiter Router: Add the network address of interface of Permiter that link between MGT and ENG.
3. Perimiter Router: Add default route and default-network.

Check the IP Address of S1/0 interface of MGT Router using show running-config command. (The interfaced used to connect to the ISP)

```
!
interface Serial1/0
ip address 198.0.18.6 255.255.255.252
!
```

For Internet sharing we have create a default route, and add default-network configuration. The IP
address is 198.0.18.6/30. Then the next hop IP will be 198.0.18.5.

ENG Router
```
ENG>enable
Password: cisco ENG# conf t
ENG(config)# no router eigrp 22
ENG(config)# router eigrp 12
ENG(config-router)# network 192.168.60.0
ENG(config-router)# network 192.168.77.0
ENG(config-router)# no auto-summary
ENG(config-router)# end
ENG# copy running-config startup-config
```

MGT Router
```
MGT>enable
Password: cisco MGT# conf t
MGT(config)# router eigrp 12
MGT(config-router)# network 192.168.77.0
MGT(config-router)# exit
```

MGT(config)# ip route 0.0.0.0 0.0.0.0 198.0.18.5
MGT(config)# ip default-network 198.0.18.0
MGT(config)# exit
MGT# copy running-config startup-config
Important:
If you refer the topology and IP chart, the MGT router uses Fa0/0 to connect ENG router, S0/0 used
to connect Remote1, and S0/1 used to connect Remote2.
Refer to the command show running-config, the command #PASSIVE-INTERFACE will deny EIGRP updates to specified interface. In that case we need to use #no passive-interface to allow the routing updates to be passed to that interface. For example when used the #show run command and we see the output like below.
!
router eigrp 22
network 192.168.77.0
network 192.168.60.0
passive-interface FastEthernet 0/0
passive-interface Serial 1/0
no auto-summary
!
Then the command would be
MGT(config)#router eigrp 12
MGT(config-router)#no passive-interface Fa0/0
MGT(config-router)#end
Also MGT router connect to the ISP router using Serial 1/0. If you see passive-interface s1/0, then
do not remove it using #no passive-interface s1/0 command.

## 100. Lab Simulation Question - CLI

Central Florida Widgets recently installed a new router in their office. Complete the network installation by performing the initial router configurations and configuring R1PV2 routing using the
router command line interface (CLI) on the RC.
Configure the router per the following requirements:
- Name of the router is R2
- Enable.secret password is cisco
- The password to access user EXEC mode using the console is cisco2
- The password to allow telnet access to the router is cisco3
IPV4 addresses mast be configured as follows:
- Ethernet network 209.165.201.0/27 - router has fourth assignable host address in subnet
- Serial network is 192.0.2.176/28 - router has last assignable host address in the subnet.
- Interfaces should be enabled.
- Router protocol is RIPV2
Attention:
In practical examinations, please note the following, the actual information will prevail.
1. Name or the router is xxx
2. EnablE. secret password is xxx

3. Password In access user EXEC mode using the console is xxx
4. The password to allow telnet access to the router is xxx
5. IP information

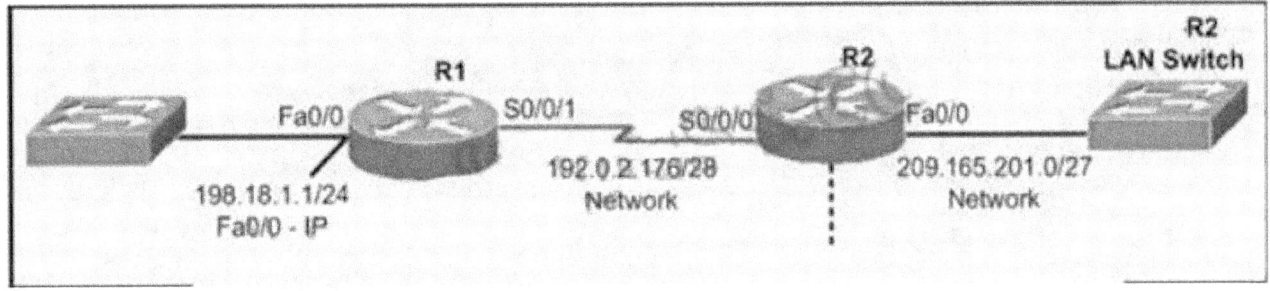

**Answer:**
Step 1:
Click on the console host, you will get a pop-up screen CLI of Router.
Router>
Configure the new router as per the requirements provided in Lab question
Requirement 1:
Name of the router is R2
Step 2:
To change the hostname of the router to R2 follow the below steps:
Router>
Router>enable
Router#configure terminal
Router(config)#hostname R2
R2(config)#
Requirement 2:
Enable-secret password is cisco1
Step 3:
To set the enable secret password to cisco1 use the following command
R2(config)#enable secret cisco1
Requirement 3:
The password to access user EXEC mode using the console is cisco2
Step 4:
We need to configure the line console 0 with the password cisco2
Also remember to type login command after setting up the password on line con 0 which allows
router to accept logins via console.
R2(config)#line con 0
R2(config-line)#password cisco2
R2(config-line)#login
R2(config-line)#exit
R2(config)#
Requirement 4:
The password to allow telnet access to the router is cisco3
Step 5:
To allow telnet access we need to configure the vty lines 0 4 with the password cisco3
Also remember to type login command after setting up the password on line vty 0 4 which

allows
router to accept logins via telnet.
R2(config)#line vty 0 4
R2(config-line)#password cisco3
R2(config-line)#login
R2(config-line)#exit
R2(config)#

Requirement 5:
(5.1) Ethernet network 209.165.201.0 /27 - Router has the fourth assignable host address in subnet.
(5.2) Serial Network is 192.0.2.176 /28 - Router has the last assignable host address in subnet.

Step 6:
Ethernet network 209.165.201.0 /27 - Router has the fourth assignable host address in subnet.
Ethernet Interface on router R2 is Fast Ethernet 0/0 as per the exhibit
First we need to identify the subnet mask
Network: 209.165.201.0 /27
Subnet mask: /27: 27 bits = 8 + 8 + 8 + 3
=8(bits).8(bits).8(bits) .11100000 (3bits)
=255.255.255.11100000
=11100000 = 128+64+32+0+0+0+0+0
= 224
Subnet mask: 255.255.255.224
Different subnet networks and there valid first and last assignable host address range for above
subnet mask are
Subnet Networks :::::: Valid Host address range :::::: Broadcast address
209.165.201.0 :::::: 209.165.201.1 - 209.165.201.30 :::::: 209.165.201.31
209.165.201.32 :::::: 209.165.201.33 - 209.165.201.62 :::::: 209.165.201.63
209.165.201.64 :::::: 209.165.201.65 - 209.165.201.94 :::::: 209.165.201.95
209.165.201.96 :::::: 209.165.201.97 - 209.165.201.126 :::::: 209.165.201.127
209.165.201.128 :::::: 209.165.201.129 - 209.165.201.158 :::::: 209.165.201.159
209.165.201.160 :::::: 209.165.201.161 - 209.165.201.190 :::::: 209.165.201.191
209.165.201.192 :::::: 209.165.201.193 - 209.165.201.222 :::::: 209.165.201.223
209.165.201.224 :::::: 209.165.201.225 - 209.165.201.254 :::::: 209.165.201.255
Use above table information for network 209.165.201.0 /27 to identify
First assignable host address: 209.165.201.1
Last assignable host address: 209.165.201.30
Fourth assignable host address: 209.165.201.4
This IP address (209.165.201.4) which we need to configure on Fast Ethernet 0/0 of the router
using the subnet mask 255.255.255.224
R2(config)#interface fa 0/0
R2(config-if)#ip address 209.165.201.4 255.255.255.224

Requirement 6:
To enable interfaces
Use no shutdown command to enable interfaces
R2(config-if)#no shutdown

R2(config-if)#exit
Step 7:
Serial Network is 192.0.2.176 /28 - Router has the last assignable host address in subnet.
Serial Interface on R2 is Serial 0/0/0 as per the exhibit
First we need to identify the subnet mask
Network: 192.0.2.176 /28
Subnet mask: /28: 28bits = 8bits+8bits+8bits+4bits
=8(bits).8(bits).8(bits) .11110000 (4bits)
=255.255.255.11100000
=11100000 = 128+64+32+16+0+0+0+0
= 240
Subnet mask: 255.255.255.240
Different subnet networks and there valid first and last assignable host address range for above
subnet mask are
Subnet Networks ::::: Valid Host address ::::::::::: Broadcast address
192.0.2.0 ::::::: 192.0.2.1 - 192.0.2.14 ::::::: 192.0.2.15
192.0.2.16 :::::::: 192.0.2.17 - 192.0.2.30 ::::::: 192.0.2.31
192.0.2.32 :::::::: 192.0.2.33 - 192.0.2.46 ::::::: 192.0.2.47
192.0.2.48 ::::::: 192.0.2.49 - 192.0.2.62 ::::::: 192.0.2.64
192.0.2.64 :::::::: 192.0.2.65 - 192.0.2.78 ::::::: 192.0.2.79
192.0.2.80 ::::::::: 192.0.2.81 - 192.0.2.94 ::::::: 192.0.2.95
192.0.2.96 ::::::: 192.0.2.97 - 192.0.2.110 ::::::: 192.0.2.111
192.0.2.112 :::::::: 192.0.2.113 - 192.0.2.126 ::::::: 192.0.2.127
192.0.2.128 ::::::::: 192.0.2.129 - 192.0.2.142 ::::::: 192.0.2.143
192.0.2.144 ::::::: 192.0.2.145 - 192.0.2.158 ::::::: 192.0.2.159
192.0.2.160 :::::::: 192.0.2.161 - 192.0.2.174 ::::::: 192.0.2.175
192.0.2.176 :::::::: 192.0.2.177 - 192.0.2.190 ::::::: 192.0.2.191
and so on ….
Use above table information for network 192.0.2.176 /28 to identify
First assignable host address: 192.0.2.177
Last assignable host address: 192.0.2.190
We need to configure Last assignable host address (192.0.2.190) on serial 0/0/0 using the subnet
mask 255.255.255.240
R2(config)#interface serial 0/0/0
R2(config-if)#ip address 192.0.2.190 255.255.255.240
Requirement 6:
To enable interfaces
Use no shutdown command to enable interfaces
R2(config-if)#no shutdown
R2(config-if)#exit
Requirement 7:
Router protocol is RIPv2
Step 8:
Need to enable RIPv2 on router and advertise its directly connected networks
R2(config)#router rip
To enable RIP v2 routing protocol on router use the command version 2
R2(config-router)#version 2

Optional: no auto-summary (Since LAB networks do not have discontinuous networks)
RIP v2 is classless, and advertises routes including subnet masks, but it summarizes routes by
default.
So the first things we need to do when configuring RIP v2 is turn off auto-summarization with the
router command no auto-summary if you must perform routing between disconnected subnets.
R2 (config-router) # no auto-summary
Advertise the serial 0/0/0 and fast Ethernet 0/0 networks into RIP v2 using network command
R2(config-router)#network 192.0.2.176
R2(config-router)#network 209.165.201.0
R2(config-router)#end
Step 9:
Important please do not forget to save your running-config to startup-config
R2# copy running-config startup-config

**101. Lab Simulation Question - ACL-4**

A network associate is adding security to the configuration of the Corp1 router. The user on host C should be able to use a web browser to access financial information from the Finance Web Server. No other hosts from the LAN nor the Core should be able to use a web browser to access this server. Since there are multiple resources for the corporation at this location including other resources on the Finance Web Server, all other traffic should be allowed.

The task is to create and apply an access-list with no more than three statements that will allow ONLY host C web access to the Finance Web Server. No other hosts will have web access to the Finance Web Server. All other traffic is permitted.

Access to the router CLI can be gained by clicking on the appropriate host.

All passwords have been temporarily set to "cisco7".
The Core connection uses an IP address of 198.18.196.65
The computers in the hosts LAN have been assigned addresses of 192.168.33.1 - 192.168.33.254.
- host A 192.168.33.1
- host B 192.168.33.2
- host C 192.168.33.3
- host D 192.168.33.4

The servers in the Server LAN have been assigned addresses of 172.22.242.17 - 172.22.242.30
The Finance Web Server is assigned an IP address of 172.22.242.23

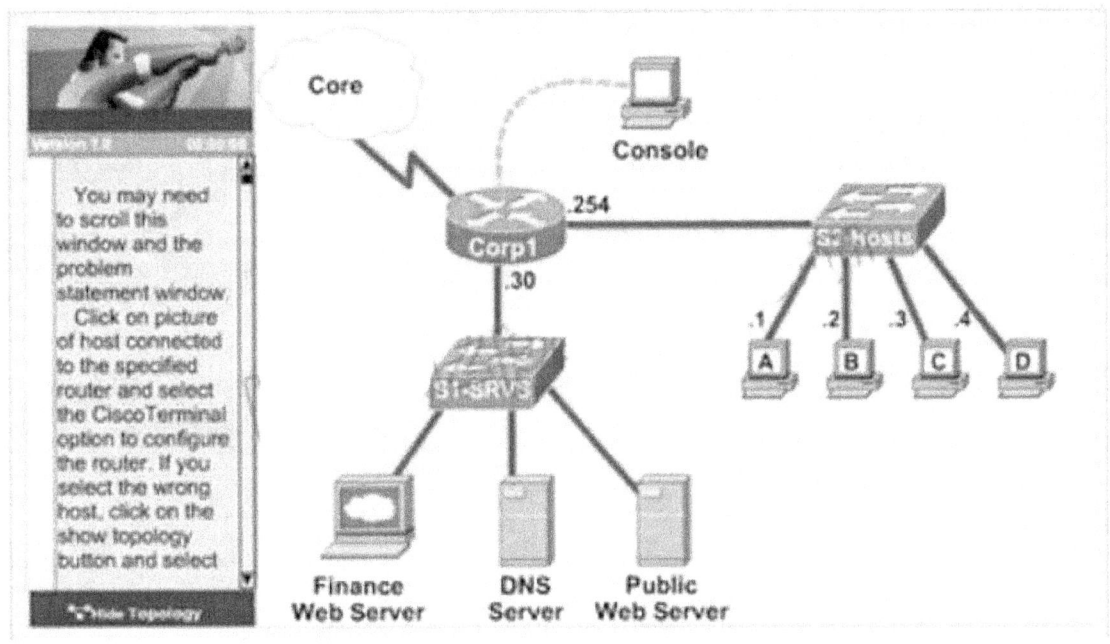

**Answer:**
Corp1>enable
Corp1#configure terminal
Corp1(config)#access-list 100 permit tcp host 192.168.33.3 host 172.22.242.23 eq 80
Corp1(config)#access-list 100 deny tcp any host 172.22.242.23 eq 80
Corp1(config)#access-list 100 permit ip any any
Corp1(config)#interface fa 0/1 sh ip int brief
Corp1(config-if)#ip access-group 100 out
Corp1(config-if)#end
Corp1#copy running-config startup-config
Explanation:
Select the console on Corp1 router
Configuring ACL
Corp1>enable
Corp1#configure terminal
Comment: To permit only Host C (192.168.33.3){source addr} to access finance server address
(172.22.242.23) {destination addr} on port number 80 (web)
Corp1(config)#access-list 100 permit tcp host 192.168.33.3 host 172.22.242.23 eq 80
Comment: To deny any source to access finance server address (172.22.242.23) {destination addr}
on port number 80 (web)
Corp1(config)#access-list 100 deny tcp any host 172.22.242.23 eq 80
Comment: To permit ip protocol from any source to access any destination because of the implicit
deny any any statement at the end of ACL.
Corp1(config)#access-list 100 permit ip any any
Applying the ACL on the Interface

Comment: Check show ip interface brief command to identify the interface type and number by
checking the IP address configured.
Corp1(config)#interface fa 0/1
If the ip address configured already is incorrect as well as the subnet mask. this should be corrected
in order ACL to work type this commands at interface mode :
no ip address 192.x.x.x 255.x.x.x (removes incorrect configured ipaddress and subnet mask)
Configure Correct IP Address and subnet mask:
ip address 172.22.242.30 255.255.255.240 ( range of address specified going to server is given as
172.22.242.17 - 172.22.242.30 )
Comment: Place the ACL to check for packets going outside the interface towards the finance web
server.
Corp1(config-if)#ip access-group 100 out
Corp1(config-if)#end
Important: To save your running config to startup before exit.
Corp1#copy running-config startup-config
Verifying the Configuration:
Step1: show ip interface brief command identifies the interface on which to apply access list. Step2:
Click on each host A,B,C & D . Host opens a web browser page , Select address box of the web
browser and type the ip address of finance web server(172.22.242.23) to test whether it permits
/deny access to the finance web Server .
Step 3: Only Host C (192.168.33.3) has access to the server . If the other host can also access
then maybe something went wrong in your configuration . check whether you configured correctly
and in order.
Step 4: If only Host C (192.168.33.3) can access the Finance Web Server you can click on NEXT
button to successfully submit the ACL SIM.

**102. Lab Simulation Question - ACL-2**

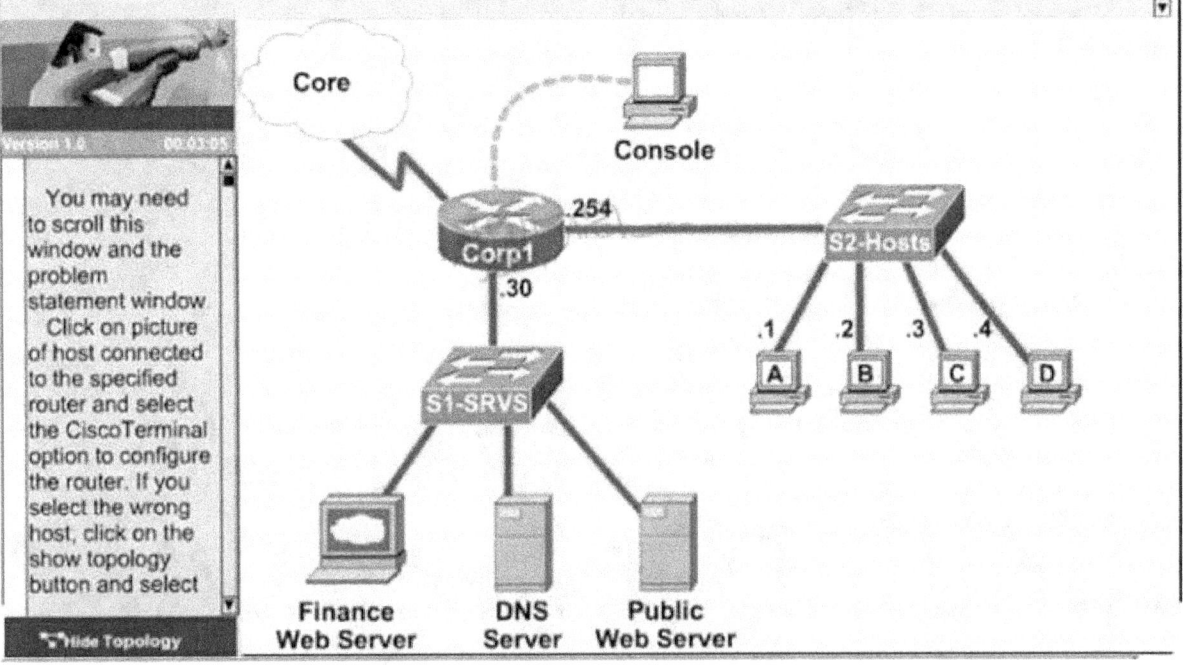

**Answer:**
Corp1#conf t
Corp1(config)# access-list 128 permit tcp host 192.168.240.1 host 172.22.141.26 eq www Corp1(config)# access-list 128 deny tcp any host 172.22.141.26 eq www
Corp1(config)# access-list 128 permit ip any any

```
Corp1(config)#int fa0/1
Corp1(config-if)#ip access-group 128 out
Corp1(config-if)#end
Corp1#copy run startup-config
```

**103. Lab Simulation Question - ACL-3**

A network associate is adding security to the configuration of the Corp1 router. The user on host C should be able to use a web browser to access financial information from the Finance Web Server. No other hosts from the LAN nor the Core should be able to use a web browser to access this server. Since there are multiple resources for the corporation at this location including other resources on the Finance Web Server, all other traffic should be allowed.

The task is to create and apply an access-list with no more than three statements that will allow ONLY host C web access to the Finance Web Server. No other hosts will have web access to the Finance Web Server. All other traffic is permitted.

Access to the router CLI can be gained by clicking on the appropriate host.

All passwords have been temporarily set to "cisco".
The Core connection uses an IP address of 198.18.196.65
The computers in the Hosts LAN have been assigned addresses of 192.168.33.1 - 192.168.33.254.
- host A 192.168.33.1
- host B 192.168.33.2
- host C 192.168.33.3
- host D 192.168.33.4

The servers in the Server LAN have been assigned addresses of 172.22.242.17 - 172.22.242.30
The Finance Web Server is assigned an IP address of 172.22.242.23

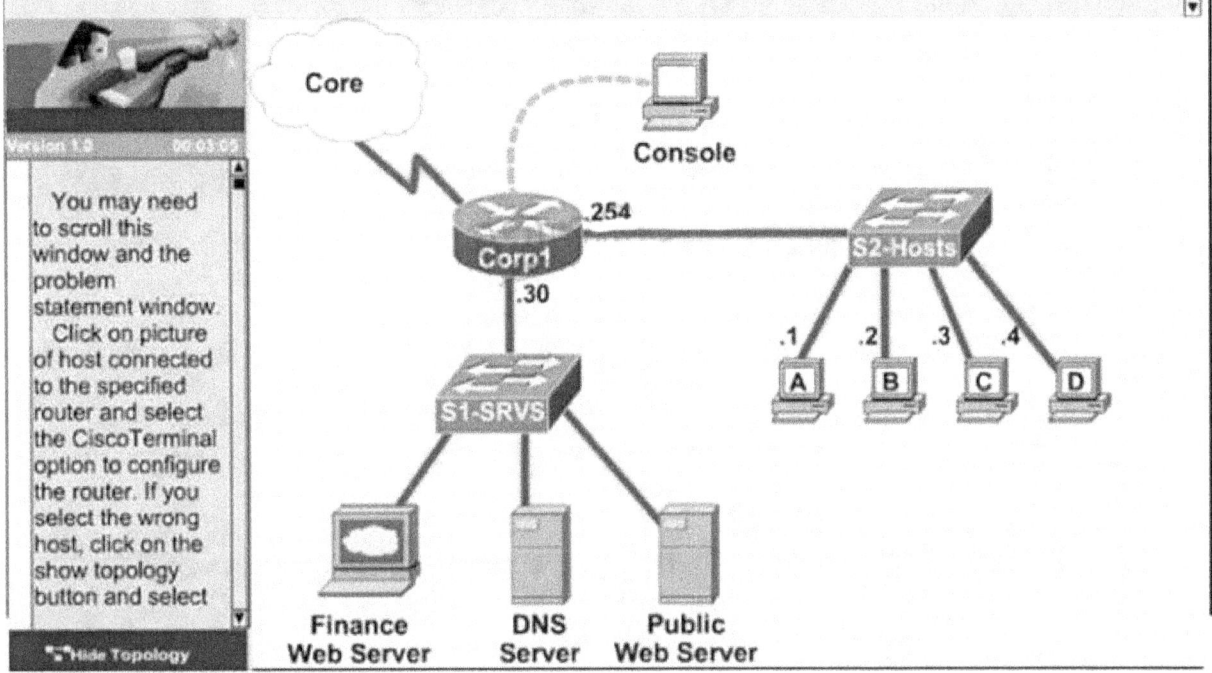

Answer:
Corp1>enable
Corp1#configure terminal
Corp1(config)#access-list 100 permit tcp host 192.168.33.3 host 172.22.242.23 eq 80
Corp1(config)#access-list 100 deny tcp 192.168.33.0 0.0.0.255 host 172.22.242.23 eq 80
Corp1(config)#access-list 100 permit ip any any
Corp1(config)#interface fa 0/1 sh ip int brief
Corp1(config-if)#ip access-group 100 out
Corp1(config-if)#end
Corp1#copy running-config startup-config
Explanation:
Select the console on Corp1 router
Configuring ACL
Corp1 >enable
Corp1#configure terminal
comment: To permit only Host C (192.168. 33. 3){source addr} to access finance server address
(172.22. 242. 23){destination addr} on port number 80 (web)
Corp1(config)#access-list 100 permit tcp host 192.168.33.3 host 172.22.242.23 eq 80

Comment: To deny any source to access finance server address (172. 22. 242. 23) {destination
addr} on port number 80 (web)
Corp1(config)#access-list 100 deny tcp any host 172.22.242.23 eq 80
Comment: To permit ip protocol from any source to access any destination because of the implicit
deny any any statement at the end of ACL.
Corp1(config)#access-list 100 permit ip any any
Applying the ACL on the Interface
comment: Check show ip interface brief command to identify the interface type and number by
checking the IP address configured.
Corp1(config)#interface fa 0/1
If the ip address configured already is incorrect as well as the subnet mask, this should be corrected
in order ACL to work type this commands at interface mode :
no ip address 192. x. x. x 255. x. x. x (removes incorrect configured ip address and subnet mask)
Configure Correct IP Address and subnet mask:
ip address 172. 22. 242. 30 255. 255. 255. 240 (range of address specified going to server is given
as 172. 22. 242. 17-172. 22. 242. 30 )
Comment: Place the ACL to check for packets going outside the interface towards the finance web
server.
Corp1(config-if)#ip access-group 100 out
Corp1(config-if)#end
Important: To save your running config to startup before exit.
Corp1#copy running-config startup- config
Verifying the Configuration:
Step1: show ip interface brief command identifies the interface on which to apply access list. Step2:
Click on each host A,B,C & D. Host opens a web browser page, Select address box of the web
browser and type the ip address of finance web server(172. 22. 242. 23) to test whether it permits
/deny access to the finance web Server.
Step 3: Only Host C (192.168. 33. 3) has access to the server. If the other host can also access
then maybe something went wrong in your configuration check whether you configured correctly
and in order.
Step 4: If only Host C (192.168. 33. 3) can access the Finance Web Server you can click on NEXT
button to successfully submit the ACL SIM.

**104. Lab Simulation Question - NAT-1**

The following have already been configured on the router:
- The basic router configuration
- The appropriate interfaces have been configured for NAT inside and NAT outside.
- The appropriate static routes have also been configured (since the company will be a stub network, no routing protocol will be required)
- All passwords have been temporarily set to "cisco".

The task is to complete the NAT configuration using all IP addresses assigned by the ISP to provide Internet access for the hosts in the Weaver LAN. Functionality can be tested by clicking on the host provided for testing.

Configuration information
  router name - Weaver
  inside global addresses-198.18.184.105 198.18.184.110/29
  inside local addresses - 192.168.100.17 - 192.168.100.30/28
  number of inside hosts - 14

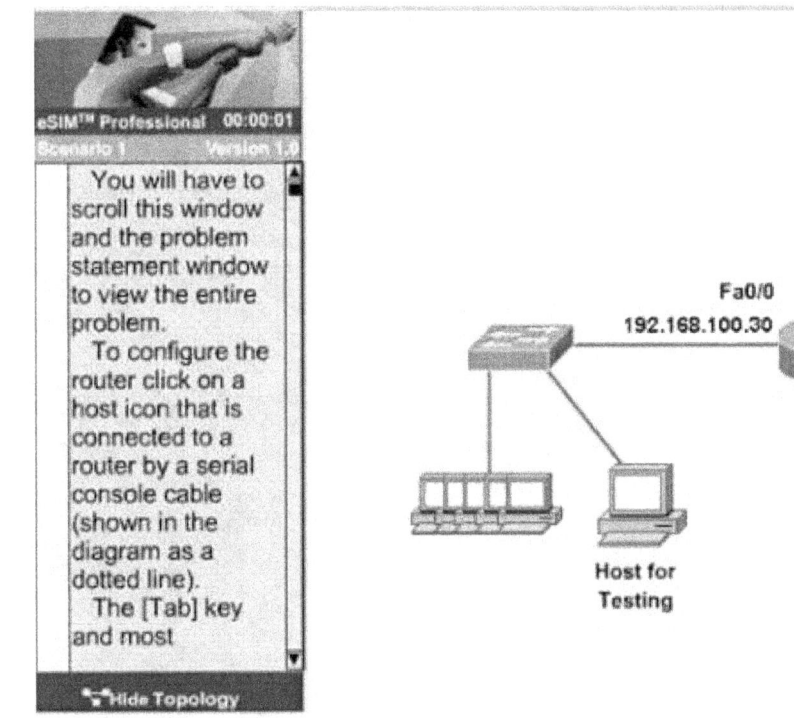

A network associate is configuring a router for the weaver company to provide internet access. The ISP has provided the company six public IP addresses of 198.18.184.105 198.18.184.110. The company has 14 hosts that need to access the internet simultaneously. The hosts in the company LAN have been assigned private space addresses in the range of 192.168.100.17 ?192.168.100.30.

Answer:
The company has 14 hosts that need to access the internet simultaneously but we just have 6
public IP addresses from 198.18.184.105 to 198.18.184.110/29.
Therefore we have to use NAT overload (or PAT)

Double click on the Weaver router to open it
Router>enable
Router#configure terminal
First you should change the router's name to Weaver
Router(config)#hostname Weaver
Create a NAT pool of global addresses to be allocated with their netmask.
Weaver(config)#ip nat pool mypool 198.18.184.105 198.18.184.110 netmask 255.255.255.248
Create a standard access control list that permits the addresses that are to be translated
Weaver(config)#access-list 1 permit 192.168.100.16 0.0.0.15
Establish dynamic source translation, specifying the access list that was defined in the prior step
Weaver(config)#ip nat inside source list 1 pool mypool overload
This command translates all source addresses that pass access list 1, which means a source
address from 192.168.100.17 to 192.168.100.30, into an address from the pool named mypool (the
pool contains addresses from 198.18.184.105 to 198.18.184.110)
Overload keyword allows to map multiple IP addresses to a single registered IP address (many-to-
one) by using different ports
The question said that appropriate interfaces have been configured for NAT inside and NAT outside
statements.
This is how to configure the NAT inside and NAT outside, just for your understanding:
Weaver(config)#interface fa0/0
Weaver(config-if)#ip nat inside
Weaver(config-if)#exit
Weaver(config)#interface s0/0
Weaver(config-if)#ip nat outside
Weaver(config-if)#end
Finally, we should save all your work with the following command:
Weaver#copy running-config startup-config
Check your configuration by going to "Host for testing" and type:
C :\>ping 192.0.2.114
The ping should work well and you will be replied from 192.0.2.114

**105.** Lab Simulation Question - NAT-2 A network associate is configuring a router for the Weaver company to provide internet access. The ISP has provided the company six public IP addresses of 198.18.184.105 - 198.18.184.110. The company has 14 hosts that need to access the internet simultaneously. The hosts in the company LAN have been assigned private space addresses in the range of 192.168.100.17 – 192.168.100.30.

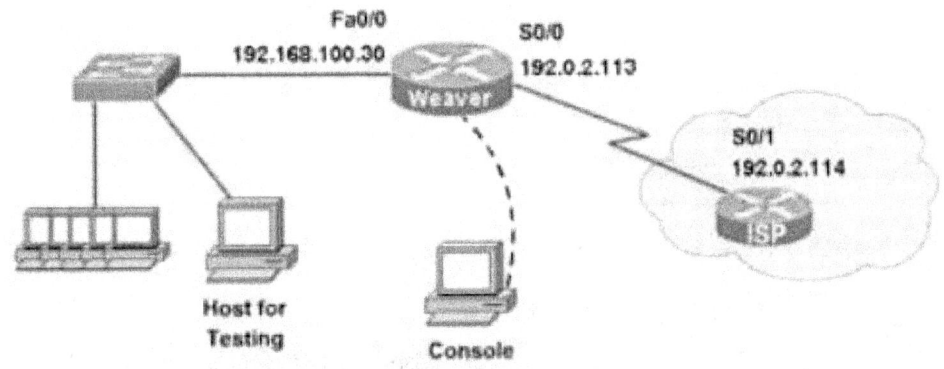

The following have already been configured on the router:
The basic router configuration
The appropriate interfaces have been configured for NAT inside and NAT outside
The appropriate static routes have also been configured (since the company will be a stub network, no routing protocol will be required.)
All passwords have been temporarily set to "cisco"
The task is to complete the NAT configuration using all IP addresses assigned by the ISP to provide
internet access for the hosts in the weaver LAN. Functionality can be tested by clicking on the host
provided for testing.
Configuration information:
Router name - Weaver
Inside global addresses - 198.18.184.105 – 198.18.184.110 /29
Inside local addresses - 192.168.100.17 – 192.168.100.30 /28

Number of inside hosts - 14
Answer:
Step 1: Router Name
Router>enable
Router#configure terminal
Router(config)#hostname Weaver
Weaver(config)#
Step 2: NAT Configuration
Weaver(config)#access-list 10 permit 192.168.100.16 0.0.0.15
Weaver(config)#ip nat pool mynatpool 198.18.184.105 198.18.184.110 netmask 255.255.255.248
Weaver(config)#ip nat inside source list 10 pool mynatpool overload
Weaver(config)#end
Step 3: Save Configuration
Weaver#copy run start
Verification:
We can verify the answer by pinging the ISP IP Address (192.0.2.114) from Host for testing.
Click "Host for testing"
In command prompt, type "ping 192.0.2.114". If ping succeeded then the NAT is working

properly.
Screen Shots:

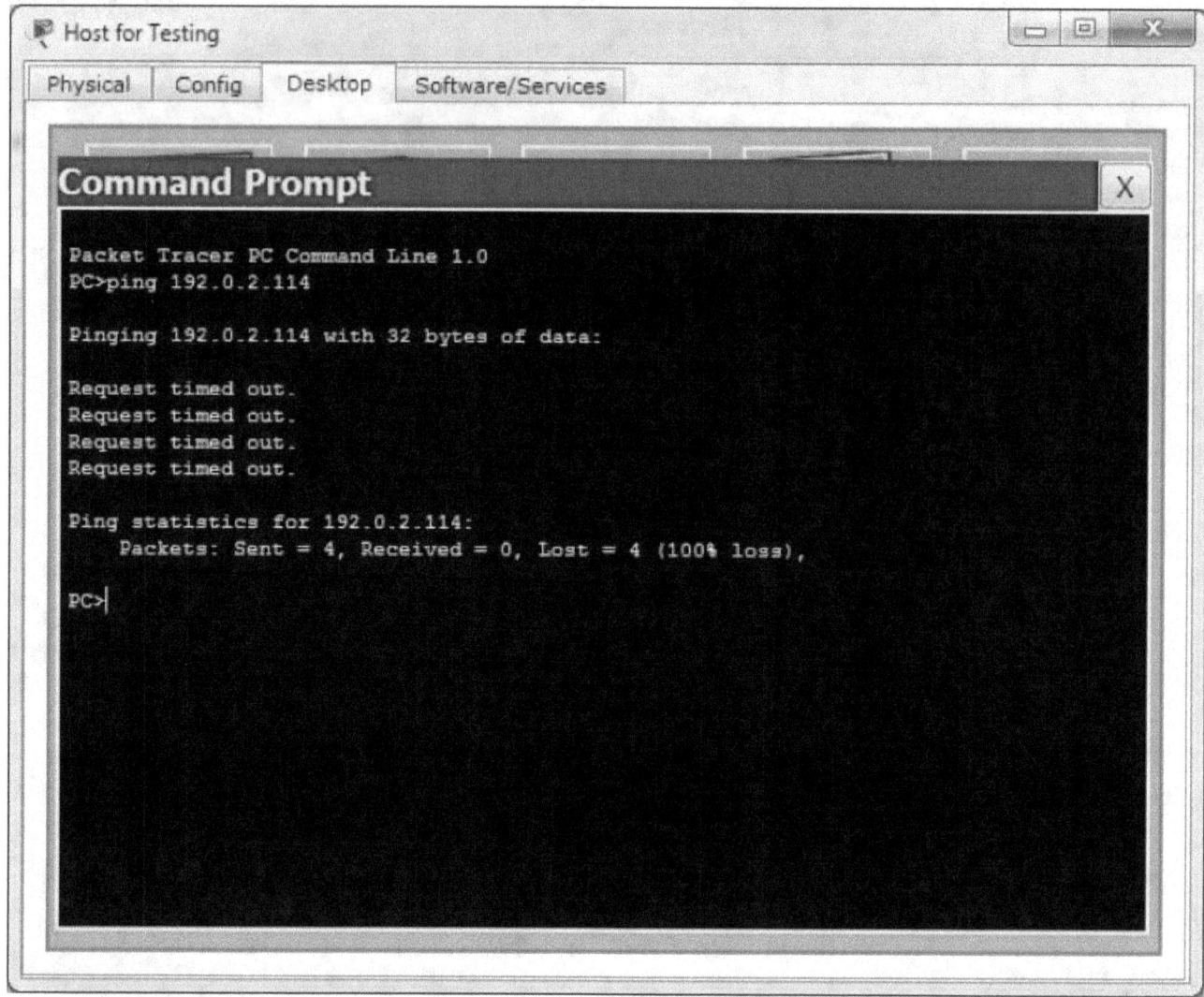

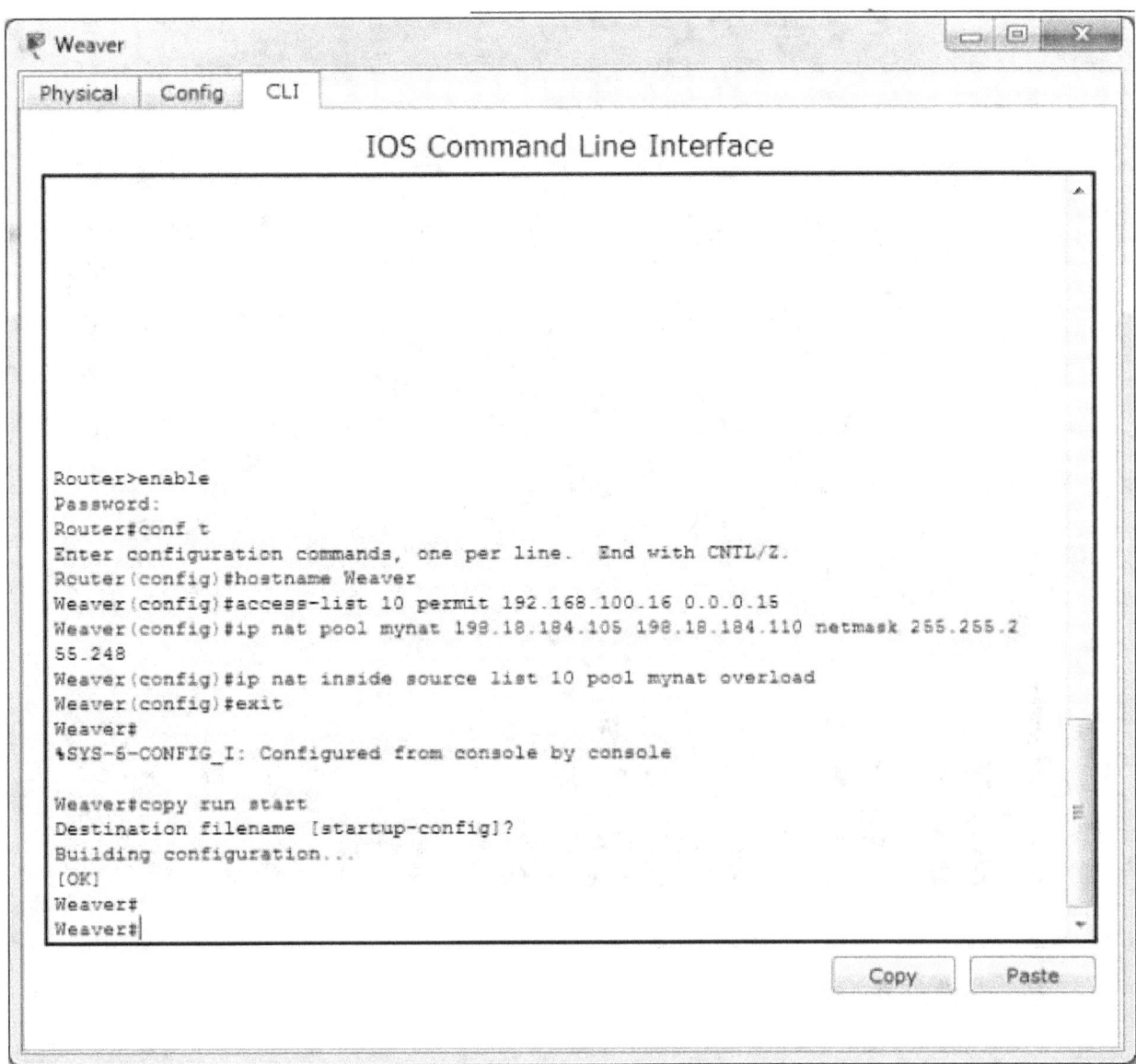

**106. In a switched environment, what does the IEEE 802.1Q standard describe?**

A. the operation of VTP
B. a method of VLAN trunking
C. an approach to wireless LAN communication
D. the process for root bridge selection
E. VLAN pruning

**Answer: B**
**Explanation:**
A broadcast domain must sometimes exist on more than one switch in the network. To accomplish
this, one switch must send frames to another switch and indicate which VLAN a particular frame
belongs to. On Cisco switches, a trunk link is created to accomplish this VLAN identification. ISL
and IEEE 802.1Q are different methods of putting a VLAN identifier in a Layer 2 frame. The IEEE
802.1Q protocol interconnects VLANs between multiple switches, routers, and servers. With

802.1Q, a network administrator can define a VLAN topology to span multiple physical devices.
Cisco switches support IEEE 802.1Q for FastEthernet and Gigabit Ethernet interfaces. An 802.1Q
trunk link provides VLAN identification by adding a 4-byte tag to an Ethernet Frame as it leaves a
trunk port.

**107. What are three benefits of GLBP? (Choose three.)**
A. GLBP supports up to eight virtual forwarders per GLBP group.
B. GLBP supports clear text and MD5 password authentication between GLBP group members.
C. GLBP is an open source standardized protocol that can be used with multiple vendors.
D. GLBP supports up to 1024 virtual routers.
E. GLBP can load share traffic across a maximum of four routers.
F. GLBP elects two AVGs and two standby AVGs for redundancy.

Answer: BDE

**108. Which three statements about HSRP operation are true? (Choose three.)**

A. The virtual IP address and virtual MA+K44C address are active on the HSRP Master router.
B. The HSRP default timers are a 3 second hello interval and a 10 second dead interval.
C. HSRP supports only clear-text authentication.
D. The HSRP virtual IP address must be on a different subnet than the routers' interfaces on the same LAN.
E. The HSRP virtual IP address must be the same as one of the router's interface addresses on the LAN.
F. HSRP supports up to 255 groups per interface, enabling an administrative form of load balancing.

Answer: ABF
Explanation:
The virtual MAC address of HSRP version 1 is 0000.0C07.ACxx, where xx is the HSRP group
number in hexadecimal based on the respective interface. For example, HSRP group 10 uses the
HSRP virtual MAC address of 0000.0C07.AC0A. HSRP version 2 uses a virtual MAC address of
0000.0C9F.FXXX (XXX: HSRP group in hexadecimal)

**109. Which three statements about Syslog utilization are true? (Choose three.)**

A. Utilizing Syslog improves network performance.
B. The Syslog server automatically notifies the network administrator of network problems.
C. A Syslog server provides the storage space necessary to store log files without using router disk space.
D. There are more Syslog messages available within Cisco IOS than there are comparable

SNMP trap messages.
E. Enabling Syslog on a router automatically enables NTP for accurate time stamping.
F. A Syslog server helps in aggregation of logs and alerts.

Answer: CDF

110. A network administrator enters the following command on a router: logging trap 3. What are three message types that will be sent to the Syslog server? (Choose three.)

A. informational
B. emergency
C. warning
D. critical
E. debug
F. error

Answer: BDF

111. What is the default Syslog facility level?

A. local4
B. local5
C. local6
D. local7

Answer: D

112. What command instructs the device to timestamp Syslog debug messages in milliseconds?

A. service timestamps log datetime localtime
B. service timestamps debug datetime msec
C. service timestamps debug datetime localtime
D. service timestamps log datetime msec

Answer:    B
Explanation:
The "service timestamps debug" command configures the system to apply a time stamp to debugging messages. The time-stamp format for datetime is MMM DD HH:MM:SS, where MMM is the month, DD is the date, HH is the hour (in 24-hour notation), MM is the minute, and SS is the second. With the additional keyword msec, the system includes milliseconds in the time stamp, in the format HH:DD:MM:SS.mmm, where .mmm is milliseconds

113. Refer to the exhibit. What is the cause of the Syslog output messages?

```
*Mar 01, 00:37:57.3737: %SYS-5-CONFIG_I: Configured from console by console
%LINK-5-CHANGED: Interface FastEthernet0/1, changed state to administratively down
%LINEPROTO-5-UPDOWN: Line protocol on Interface FastEthernet0/1, changed state to down
%DUAL-5-NBRCHANGE: IP-EIGRP 1: Neighbor 10.10.11.2 (FastEthernet0/1) is down: interface down
```

A. The EIGRP neighbor on Fa0/1 went down due to a failed link.
B. The EIGRP neighbor connected to Fa0/1 is participating in a different EIGRP process, causing the adjacency
to go down.
C. A shut command was executed on interface Fa0/1, causing the EIGRP adjacency to go down.
D. Interface Fa0/1 has become error disabled, causing the EIGRP adjacency to go down.

Answer: C

114. What are three components that comprise the SNMP framework? (Choose three.)

A. MIB
B. agent
C. set
D. AES
E. supervisor
F. manager

Answer: ABF

115. What are three components that comprise the SNMP framework? (Choose three.)

A. MIB
B. agent
C. set
D. AES
E. supervisor
F. manager

Answer: ABF

116. What SNMP message alerts the manager to a condition on the network?

A. response
B. get
C. trap
D. capture

Answer: C

B. To authorize user network access.
C. To report and alert link up / down instances.
D. To diagnose slow network performance, bandwidth hogs, and bandwidth utilization.
E. To detect suboptimal routing in the network.
F. To confirm the appropriate amount of bandwidth that has been allocated to each Class of Service.

**Answer: ADF**

**117. What Netflow component can be applied to an interface to track IPv4 traffic?**

A. flow monitor
B. flow record
C. flow sampler
D. flow exporter

**Answer: A**
**Explanation:**
Flow monitors are the Flexible NetFlow component that is applied to interfaces to perform network
traffic monitoring. Flow monitors consist of a record and a cache. You add the record to the flow monitor after youcreate the flow monitor. The flow monitor cache is automatically created at the
time the flow monitor is applied to the first interface. Flow data is collected from the network traffic during the monitoring process based on the key and nonkey fields in the record, which is configured for the flow monitor and stored in the flow monitor cache. For example, the following example creates a flow monitor named FLOW-MONITOR-1 and enters Flexible NetFlow flow monitor configuration mode: Router(config)# flow monitor FLOW-MONITOR-1 Router(config-flow-monitor)#

**118. What Cisco IOS feature can be enabled to pinpoint an application that is causing slow network performance?**

A. SNMP
B. Netflow
C. WCCP
D. IP SLA

Answer: B

**119. What command visualizes the general NetFlow data on the command line?**

A. show ip flow export
B. show ip flow top-talkers
C. show ip cache flow
D. show mls sampling
E. show mls netflow ip

Answer: C
Explanation:
The "show ip cache flow" command displays a summary of the NetFlow

```
GATEWAY#show ip cache flow
IP packet size distribution (1149 total packets):
   1-32   64    96   128   160   192   224   256   288   320   352   384   416   448   480
   .000  .134  .475  .100  .010  .006  .037  .043  .005  .001  .004  .001  .002  .001  .000

    512   544   576  1024  1536  2048  2560  3072  3584  4096  4608
   .003  .000  .001  .020  .147  .000  .000  .000  .000  .000  .000

IP Flow Switching Cache, 278544 bytes
  13 active, 4083 inactive, 378 added
  7046 ager polls, 0 flow alloc failures
  Active flows timeout in 30 minutes
  Inactive flows timeout in 15 seconds
IP Sub Flow Cache, 21640 bytes
  13 active, 1011 inactive, 378 added, 378 added to flow
  0 alloc failures, 0 force free
  1 chunk, 1 chunk added
  last clearing of statistics never
Protocol         Total    Flows   Packets Bytes  Packets Active(Sec) Idle(Sec)
--------         Flows    /Sec    /Flow   /Pkt   /Sec    /Flow       /Flow
TCP-WWW          32       0.0     8       989    0.1     3.8         8.1
TCP-other        24       0.0     2       57     0.0     2.2         14.4
UDP-other        309      0.1     2       105    0.3     2.4         15.4
Total:           365      0.1     3       318    0.4     2.5         14.7

SrcIf      SrcIPaddress     DstIf     DstIPaddress       Pr SrcP DstP  Pkts
Fa0/0      10.0.0.23        Null      10.255.255.255     11 0089 0089     9
Fa0/0      10.0.0.30        Null      10.255.255.255     11 008A 008A     1
```

120. What are three values that must be the same within a sequence of packets for Netflow to consider them a network flow? (Choose three.)

A. source IP address
B. source MAC address
C. egress interface
D. ingress interface
E. destination IP address
F. IP next-hop

Answer: ADE

121. Refer to the exhibit. A network administrator is configuring an EtherChannel between SW1 and SW2. The SW1 configuration is shown. What is the correct configuration for SW2?

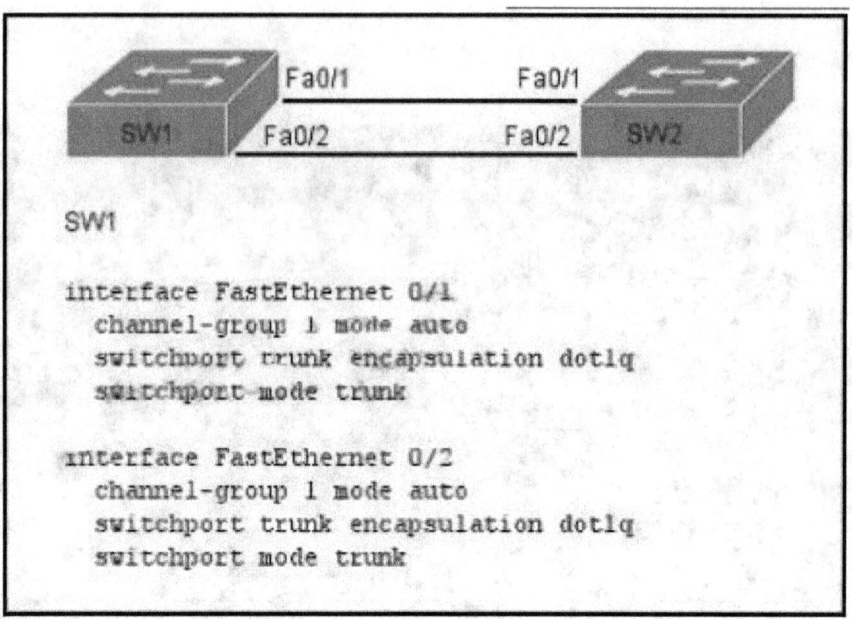

A. interface FastEthernet 0/1
channel-group 1 mode active
switchport trunk encapsulation dot1q
switchport mode trunk
interface FastEthernet 0/2
channel-group 1 mode active
switchport trunk encapsulation dot1q
switchport mode trunk

B. interface FastEthernet 0/1
channel-group 2 mode auto
switchport trunk encapsulation dot1q
switchport mode trunk
interface FastEthernet 0/2
channel-group 2 mode auto
switchport trunk encapsulation dot1q
switchport mode trunk

C. interface FastEthernet 0/1
channel-group 1 mode desirable
switchport trunk encapsulation dot1q
switchport mode trunk
interface FastEthernet 0/2
channel-group 1 mode desirable
switchport trunk encapsulation dot1q
switchport mode trunk

D. interface FastEthernet 0/1
channel-group 1 mode passive
switchport trunk encapsulation dot1q

switchport mode trunk
interface FastEthernet 0/2
channel-group 1 mode passive
switchport trunk encapsulation dot1q
switchport mode trunk

Answer: C

122. What are three factors a network administrator must consider before implementing Netflow in the network? (Choose three.)

A. CPU utilization
B. where Netflow data will be sent
C. number of devices exporting Netflow data
D. port availability
E. SNMP version
F. WAN encapsulation

Answer: ABC

123. Which two statements about the OSPF Router ID are true? (Choose two.)

A. It identifies the source of a Type 1 LSA.
B. It should be the same on all routers in an OSPF routing instance.
C. By default, the lowest IP address on the router becomes the OSPF Router ID.
D. The router automatically chooses the IP address of a loopback as the OSPF Router ID.
E. It is created using the MAC Address of the loopback interface.

Answer: AD

124. What parameter can be different on ports within an EtherChannel?

A. speed
B. DTP negotiation settings
C. trunk encapsulation
D. duplex

Answer: B

125. What are two benefits of using a single OSPF area network design? (Choose two.)

A. It is less CPU intensive for routers in the single area.
B. It reduces the types of LSAs that are generated.
C. It removes the need for virtual links.
D. It increases LSA response times.
E. It reduces the number of required OSPF neighbor adjacencies.

Answer: BC

**126. Refer to the exhibit. What set of commands was configured on interface Fa0/3 to produce the given output?**

```
FastEthernet0/3:
Port state     = 1
Channel group  = 2        Mode = Passive         Gcchange = -
Port-channel   = Po2      GC   = -               Pseudo port-channel = Po2
Port index     = 0        Load = 0x00            Protocol =   LACP
```

A. interface FastEthernet 0/3
channel-group 1 mode desirable
switchport trunk encapsulation dot1q
switchport mode trunk

B. interface FastEthernet 0/3
channel-group 2 mode passive
switchport trunk encapsulation dot1q
switchport mode trunk

C. interface FastEthernet 0/3
channel-group 2 mode active
switchport trunk encapsulation dot1q
switchport mode trunk

D. interface FastEthernet 0/3
channel-group 2 mode on
switchport trunk encapsulation dot1q
switchport mode trunk

Answer: B

**127. Refer to the exhibit. If the devices produced the given output, what is the cause of the EtherChannel problem?**

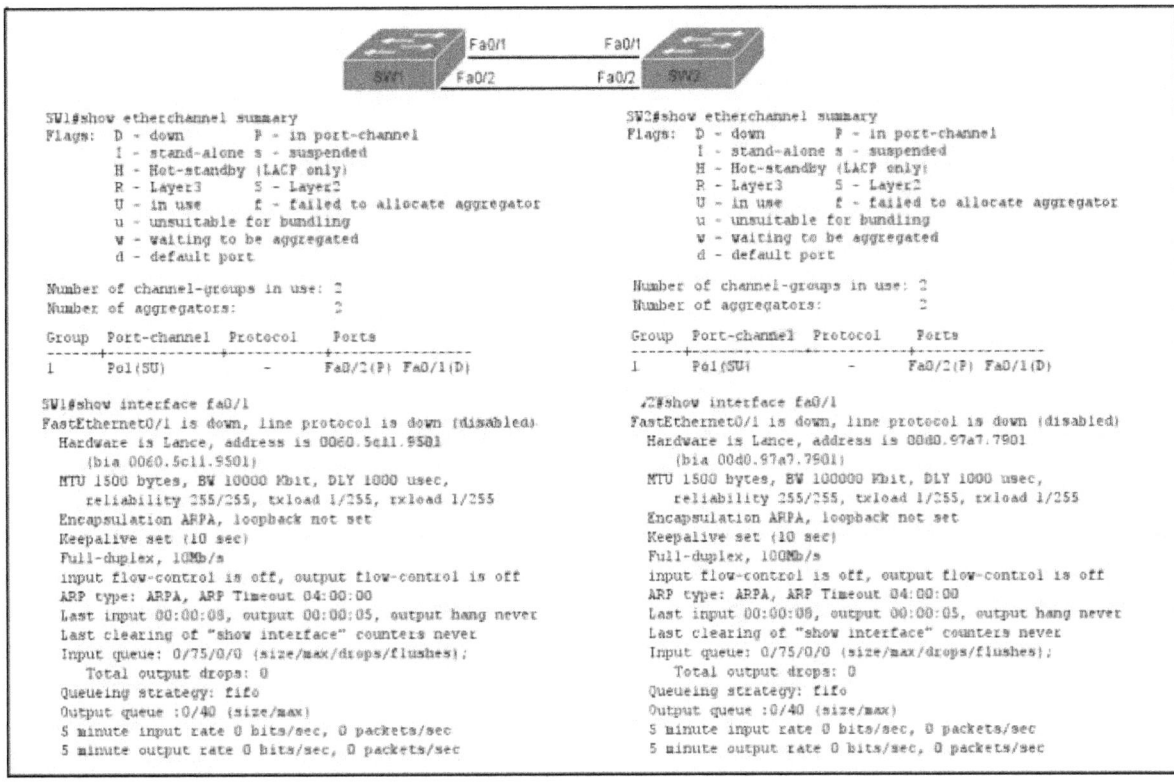

A. SW1's Fa0/1 interface is administratively shut down.
B. There is an encapsulation mismatch between SW1's Fa0/1 and SW2's Fa0/1 interfaces.
C. There is an MTU mismatch between SW1's Fa0/1 and SW2's Fa0/1 interfaces.
D. There is a speed mismatch between SW1's Fa0/1 and SW2's Fa0/1 interfaces.

Answer: D

128. What are two enhancements that OSPFv3 supports over OSPFv2? (Choose two.)

A. It requires the use of ARP.
B. It can support multiple IPv6 subnets on a single link.
C. It supports up to 2 instances of OSPFv3 over a common link.
D. It routes over links rather than over networks.

Answer: BD

129. When a router undergoes the exchange protocol within OSPF, in what order does it pass through each state?

A. exstart state > loading state > exchange state > full state
B. exstart state > exchange state > loading state > full state
C. exstart state > full state > loading state > exchange state
D. loading state > exchange state > full state > exstart state

Answer: B

130. A network administrator creates a layer 3 EtherChannel, bundling four interfaces into channel group 1. On what interface is the IP address configured?

A. the port-channel 1 interface
B. the highest number member interface
C. all member interfaces
D. the lowest number member interface

Answer: A

131. Refer to the exhibit. If the router Cisco returns the given output and has not had its router ID set manually, what value will OSPF use as its router ID?

```
Cisco#show ip interface brief
Interface           IP-Address      OK? Method Status                Protocol

FastEthernet0/0     192.168.1.1     YES manual up                    up

FastEthernet0/1     172.16.1.1      YES manual up                    up

Loopback0           1.1.1.1         YES manual up                    up

Loopback1           2.2.2.2         YES manual up                    up

Vlan1               unassigned      YES unset  administratively down down
```

A. 192.168.1.1
B. 172.16.1.1
C. 1.1.1.1
D. 2.2.2.2

Answer: D

132. What command sequence will configure a router to run OSPF and add network 10.1.1.0 /24 to area 0?

A. router ospf area 0
network 10.1.1.0 255.255.255.0 area 0

B. router ospf
network 10.1.1.0 0.0.0.255

C. router ospf 1
network 10.1.1.0 0.0.0.255 area 0

D. router ospf area 0
network 10.1.1.0 0.0.0.255 area 0

E. router ospf
network 10.1.1.0 255.255.255.0 area 0

F. router ospf 1
network 10.1.1.0 0.0.0.255

Answer: C

133. What OSPF command, when configured, will include all interfaces into area 0?

A. network 0.0.0.0 255.255.255.255 area 0
B. network 0.0.0.0 0.0.0.0 area 0
C. network 255.255.255.255 0.0.0.0 area 0
D. network all-interfaces area 0

Answer: A

134. Which statement describes the process ID that is used to run OSPF on a router?

A. It is globally significant and is used to represent the AS number.
B. It is locally significant and is used to identify an instance of the OSPF database.
C. It is globally significant and is used to identify OSPF stub areas.
D. It is locally significant and must be the same throughout an area.

Answer: B

135. Which three are the components of SNMP? (Choose three)

A. MIB
B. SNMP Manager
C. SysLog Server
D. SNMP Agent
E. Set

Answer: ABD
Explanation:
SNMP is an application-layer protocol that provides a message format for communication between
SNMP managers and agents. SNMP provides a standardized framework and a common language
used for the monitoring and management of devices in a network.
The SNMP framework has three parts:
+ An SNMP manager
+ An SNMP agent
+ A Management Information Base (MIB)
The SNMP manager is the system used to control and monitor the activities of network hosts using
SNMP. The most common managing system is called a Network Management System (NMS). The

term NMS can be applied to either a dedicated device used for network management, or the applications used on such a device. A variety of network management applications are available
for use with SNMP. These features range from simple command-line applications to feature-rich
graphical user interfaces (such as the CiscoWorks2000 line of products).
The SNMP agent is the software component within the managed device that maintains the data for
the device and reports these data, as needed, to managing systems. The agent and MIB reside on
the routing device (router, access server, or switch). To enable the SNMP agent on a Cisco routing
device, you must define the relationship between the manager and the agent.
The Management Information Base (MIB) is a virtual information storage area for network management information, which consists of collections of managed objects.

**136. What are the Popular destinations for syslog messages to be saved?**

A. Flash
B. The logging buffer .RAM
C. The console terminal
D. Other terminals
E. Syslog server

**Answer: BCE**
**Explanation:**
By default, switches send the output from system messages and debug privileged EXEC commands to a logging process. The logging process controls the distribution of logging messages to various destinations, such as the logging buffer (on RAM), terminal lines (console terminal), or a UNIX syslog server, depending on your configuration. The process also sends messages to the console.

**Note:** Syslog messages can be written to a file in Flash memory although it is not a popular place
to use. We can configure this feature with the command logging file flash:filename.

**137. Syslog was configured with a level 3 trap. Which 4 types of logs would be generated (choose four)**

A. Emergencies
B. Alerts
C. Critical
D. Errors
E. Warnings

**Answer: ABCD**
**Explanation:**
The Message Logging is divided into 8 levels as listed below:
Level Keyword Description

0 emergencies System is unusable
1 alerts Immediate action is needed
2 critical Critical conditions exist
3 errors Error conditions exist
4 warnings Warning conditions exist
5 notification Normal, but significant, conditions exist 6 informational Informational messages
7 debugging Debugging messages

The highest level is level 0 (emergencies). The lowest level is level 7. If you specify a level with the
"logging console level" command, that level and all the higher levels will be displayed. For example,
by using the "logging console warnings" command, all the logging of emergencies, alerts, critical,
errors, warnings will be displayed.

**138. What are the benefit of using Netflow? (Choose three.)**
A. Network, Application & User Monitoring
B. Network Planning
C. Security Analysis
D. Accounting/Billing

Answer: ACD

**139. Which protocol can cause overload on a CPU of a managed device?**

A. Netflow
B. WCCP
C. IP SLA
D. SNMP

Answer: D
Explanation:
Sometimes, messages like this might appear in the router console:
%SNMP-3-CPUHOG: Processing [chars] of [chars]
They mean that the SNMP agent on the device has taken too much time to process a request.
You can determine the cause of high CPU use in a router by using the output of the show process
cpu command.
**Note:** A managed device is a part of the network that requires some form of monitoring and management (routers, switches, servers, workstations, printers...).

**140. What are the three things that the Netflow uses to consider the traffic to be in a same flow?**

A. IP address
B. Interface name
C. Port numbers

D. L3 protocol type
E. MAC address

**Answer: ACD**
**Explanation:**
What is an IP Flow?
Each packet that is forwarded within a router or switch is examined for a set of IP packet attributes.
These attributes are the IP packet identity or fingerprint of the packet and determine if the packet
is unique or similar to other packets. Traditionally, an IP Flow is based on a set of 5 and up to 7 IP
packet attributes.
IP Packet attributes used by NetFlow:
+ IP source address
+ IP destination address
+ Source port
+ Destination port
+ Layer 3 protocol type
+ Class of Service
+ Router or switch interface

**141. What is the alert message generated by SNMP agents called ?**

A. TRAP
B. INFORM
C. GET
D. SET

**Answer: AB**
**Explanation:**
A TRAP is a SNMP message sent from one application to another (which is typically on a remote host). Their purpose is merely to notify the other application that something has happened, has been noticed, etc. The big problem with TRAPs is that they're unacknowledged so you don't actually know if the remote application received your oh-so-important message to it. SNMPv2 PDUs fixed this by introducing the notion of an INFORM, which is nothing more than an acknowledged TRAP.

**142. What are three reasons to collect Netflow data on a company network? (Choose three.)**

A. To identify applications causing congestion.
B. To authorize user network access.
C. To report and alert link up / down instances.
D. To diagnose slow network performance, bandwidth hogs, and bandwidth utilization.
E. To detect suboptimal routing in the network.
F. To confirm the appropriate amount of bandwidth that has been allocated to each Class of Service.

Answer: ADF

143. Which three statements about the features of SNMPv2 and SNMPv3 are true? (Choose three.)

A. SNMPv3 enhanced SNMPv2 security features.
B. SNMPv3 added the Inform protocol message to SNMP.
C. SNMPv2 added the Inform protocol message to SNMP.
D. SNMPv3 added the GetBulk protocol messages to SNMP.
E. SNMPv2 added the GetBulk protocol message to SNMP.
F. SNMPv2 added the GetNext protocol message to SNMP.

Answer: ACE

144. What authentication type is used by SNMPv2?

A. HMAC-MD5
B. HMAC-SHA
C. CBC-DES
D. community strings

Answer: D

145. Which three features are added in SNMPv3 over SNMPv2?

A. Message Integrity
B. Compression
C. Authentication
D. Encryption
E. Error Detection

Answer: ACD

146. In a GLBP network, who is responsible for the arp request?

A. AVF
B. AVG
C. Active Router
D. Standby Router

Answer: B

147. What levels will be trapped if the administrator executes the command router(config)# logging trap 4 (Choose four) ?

A. Emergency
B. Notice
C. Alert

D. Error
E. Warning

**Answer: ACDE**
**Explanation:**
The Message Logging is divided into 8 levels as listed below:
Level Keyword Description
0 emergencies System is unusable
1 alerts Immediate action is needed
2 critical Critical conditions exist
3 errors Error conditions exist
4 warnings Warning conditions exist
5 notification Normal, but significant, conditions exist 6 informational Informational messages
7 debugging Debugging messages
If you specify a level with the "logging trap level" command, that level and all the higher levels will
be logged.
For example, by using the "logging trap 4 command, all the logging of emergencies, alerts, critical,
errors, warnings will be logged.

**148. Hotspot Question**

Refer to the topology. Your company has decided to connect the main office with three other remote branch offices using point-to-point serial links. You are required to troubleshoot and resolve OSPF neighbor adjacency issues between the main office and the routers located in the remote branch offices.

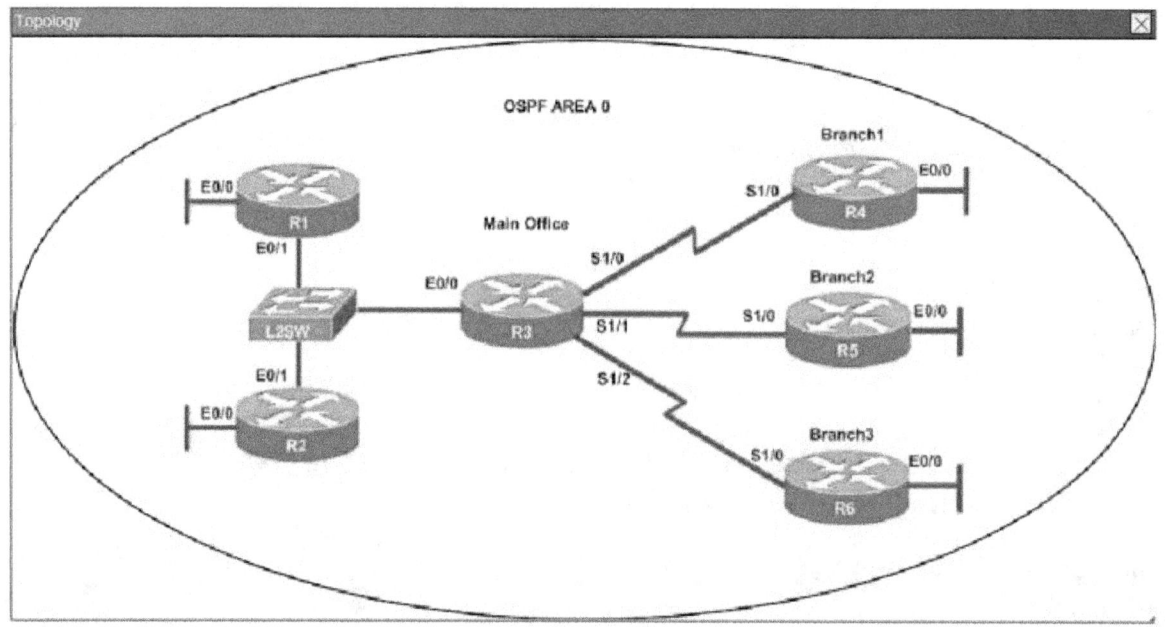

An OSPF neighbor adjacency is not formed between R3 in the main office and R4 in the Branchl office. What is causing the problem?

A. There is an area ID mismatch.
B. There is a Layer 2 issue; an encapsulation mismatch on serial links.
C. There is an OSPF hello and dead interval mismatch.
D. The R3 router ID is configured on R4.

Answer: A
Explanation:

A show running-config command on R3 and R4 shows that R4 is incorrectly configured for area 2:

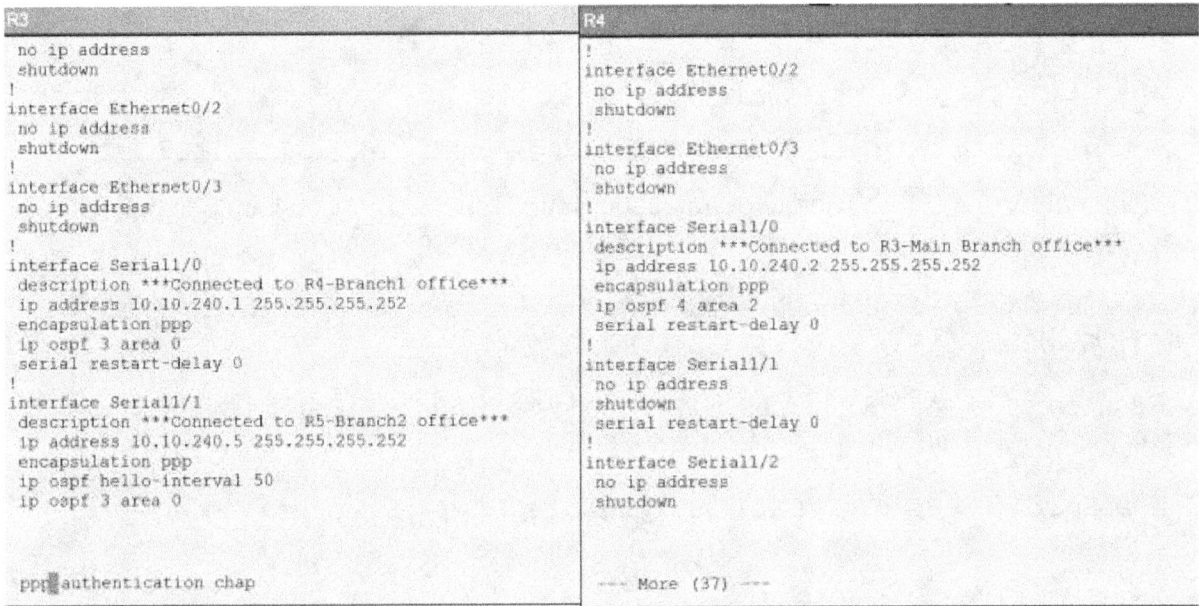

149. Hotspot Question

Refer to the topology. Your company has decided to connect the main office with three other remote
branch offices using point-to-point serial links. You are required to troubleshoot and resolve OSPF neighbor adjacency issues between the main office and the routers located in the remote branch offices.

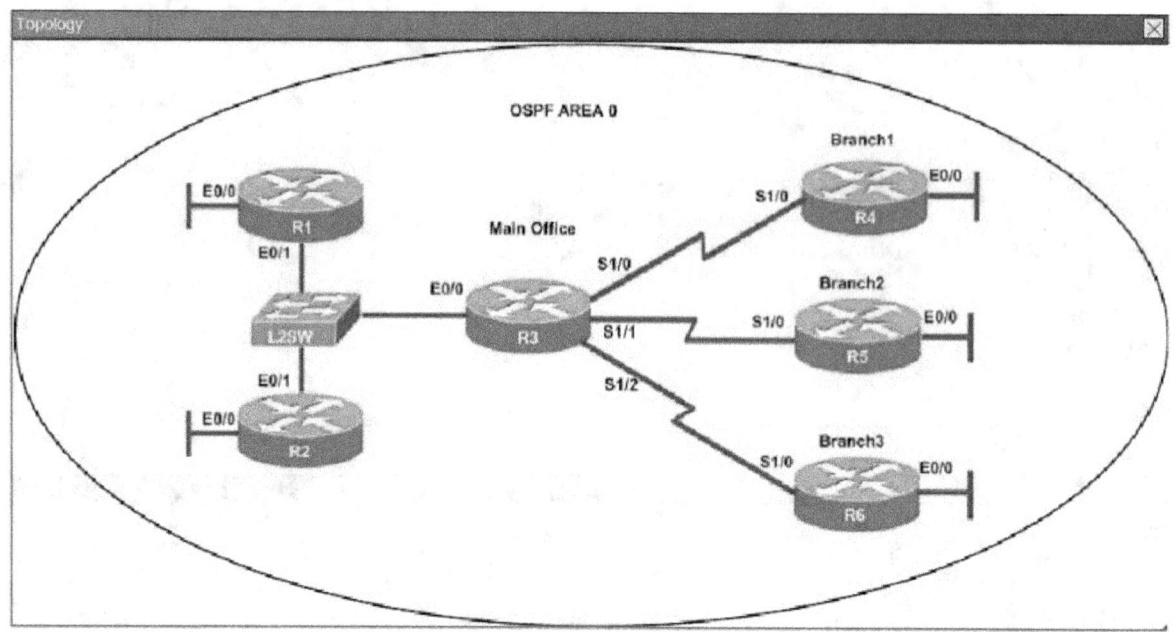

R1 does not form an OSPF neighbor adjacency with R2. Which option would fix the issue?
A. R1 ethernet0/1 is shutdown. Configure no shutdown command.

B. R1 ethernet0/1 configured with a non-default OSPF hello interval of 25: configure no ip ospf hello-interval 25

C. R2 ethernet0/1 and R3 ethernet0/0 are configured with a non-default OSPF hello interval of 25; configure no ip ospf hello-interval 25

D. Enable OSPF for R1 ethernet0/1; configure ip ospf 1 area 0 command under ethernet0/1

**Answer: B**
**Explanation:**
Looking at the configuration of R1, we see that R1 is configured with a hello interval of 25 on
interface Ethernet 0/1 while R2 is left with the default of 10 (not configured).

```
R1                                              R2
!                                               !
!                                               !
!                                               !
!                                               !
!                                               !
interface Loopback0                             interface Loopback0
 description ***Loopback***                      description ***Loopback***
 ip address 192.168.1.1 255.255.255.255          ip address 192.168.2.2 255.255.255.255
 ip ospf 1 area 0                                ip ospf 2 area 0
!                                               !
interface Ethernet0/0                           interface Ethernet0/0
 description ***Connected to R1-LAN***           description ***Connected to R2-LAN***
 ip address 10.10.110.1 255.255.255.0            ip address 10.10.120.1 255.255.255.0
 ip ospf 1 area 0                                ip ospf 2 area 0
!                                               !
interface Ethernet0/1                           interface Ethernet0/1
 description ***Connected to L2SW***             description ***Connected to L2SW***
 ip address 10.10.230.1 255.255.255.0            ip address 10.10.230.2 255.255.255.0
 ip ospf hello-interval 25                       ip ospf 2 area 0
 ip ospf 1 area 0                               !
!                                               interface Ethernet0/2
interface Ethernet0/2                            no ip address
 no ip address                                   shutdown
 shutdown


--- More (35) ---                               --- More (35) ---
```

## 150. Hotspot Question

Refer to the topology. Your company has decided to connect the main office with three other remote branch offices using point-to-point serial links. You are required to troubleshoot and resolve OSPF neighbor adjacency issues between the main office and the routers located in the remote branch offices.

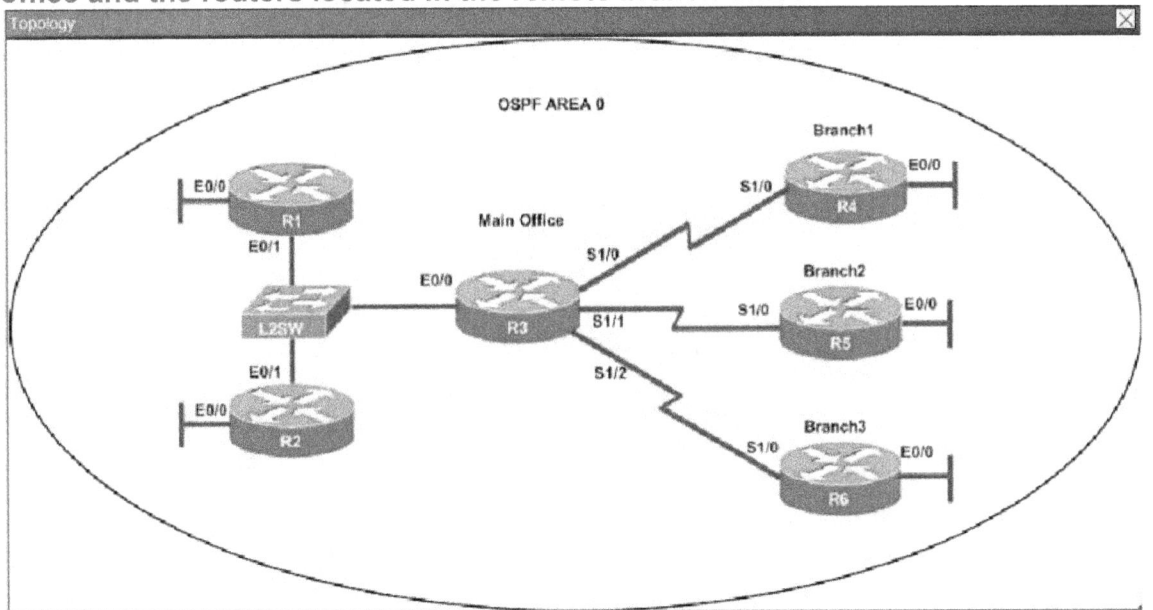

An OSPF neighbor adjacency is not formed between R3 in the main office and R6 in the Branch3 office. What is causing the problem?

A. There is an area ID mismatch.
B. There is a PPP authentication issue; the username is not configured on R3 and R6.
C. There is an OSPF hello and dead interval mismatch.
D. The R3 router ID is configured on R6.

**Answer: D**
**Explanation:**
Using the show running-config command we see that R6 has been incorrectly configured with the same router ID as R3 under the router OSPF process.

| R3 | R6 |
|---|---|
| ip address 10.10.240.5 255.255.255.252<br>encapsulation ppp<br>ip ospf hello-interval 50<br>ip ospf 3 area 0<br>ppp authentication chap<br>serial restart-delay 0<br>!<br>interface Serial1/2<br>description ***Connected to R6-Branch3 office***<br>ip address 10.10.240.9 255.255.255.252<br>encapsulation ppp<br>ip ospf 3 area 0<br>ppp authentication chap<br>serial restart-delay 0<br>!<br>interface Serial1/3<br>no ip address<br>shutdown<br>serial restart-delay 0<br>!<br>router ospf 3<br>router-id 192.168.3.3<br>!<br>ip forward-protocol nd<br>!<br>! | no ip address<br>shutdown<br>serial restart-delay 0<br>!<br>interface Serial1/2<br>no ip address<br>shutdown<br>serial restart-delay 0<br>!<br>interface Serial1/3<br>no ip address<br>shutdown<br>serial restart-delay 0<br>!<br>router ospf 6<br>router-id 192.168.3.3<br>!<br>ip forward-protocol nd<br>!<br>!<br>no ip http server<br>no ip http secure-server<br>!<br>! |

**151. Hotspot Question**

Refer to the topology. Your company has connected the routers R1. R2. and R3 with serial links.
R2 and R3 are connected to the switches SW1 and SW2, respectively. SW1 and SW2 are also
connected to the routers R4 and R5.
The EIGRP routing protocol is configured.
You are required to troubleshoot and resolve the EIGRP issues between the various routers.
Use the appropriate show commands to troubleshoot the issues.

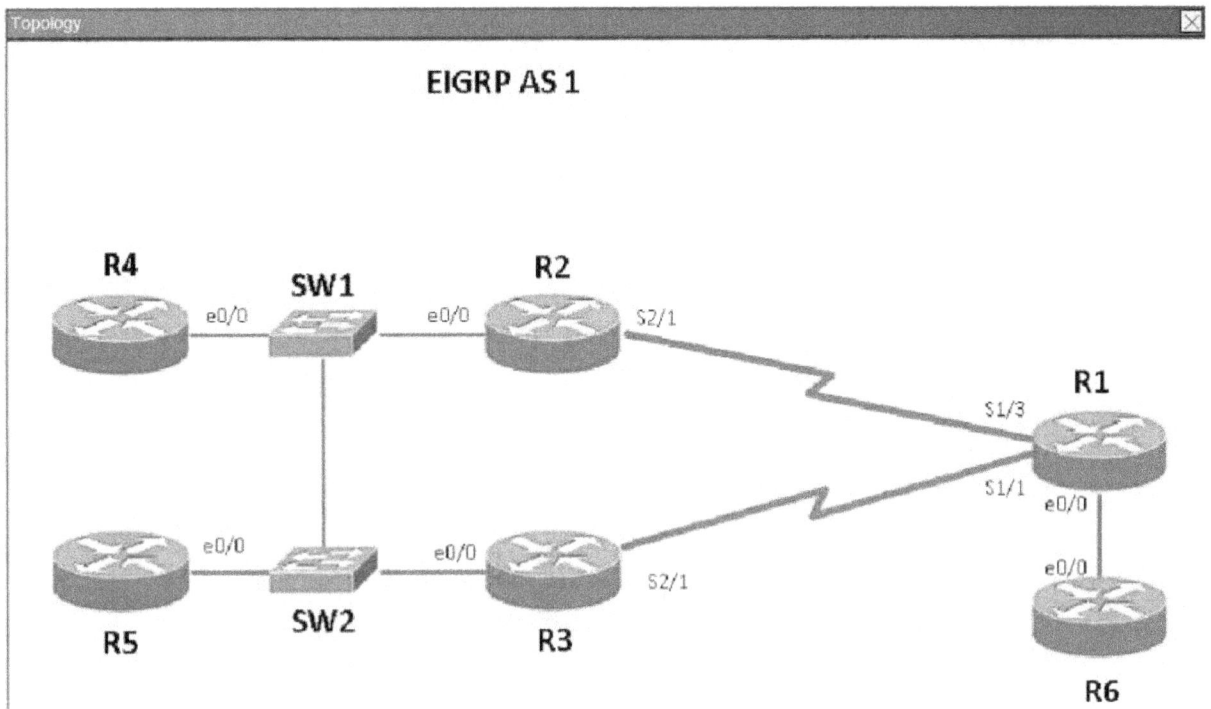

The loopback interfaces on R4 with the IP addresses of 10.4.4.4 /32, 10.4.4.5/32. and 10.4.4.6/32 are not appearing in the routing table of R5 Why are the interfaces missing?

A. The interfaces are shutdown, so they are not being advertised.
B. R4 has been incorrectly configured to be in another AS, so it does not peer with R5.
C. Automatic summarization is enabled, so only the 10.0.0.0 network is displayed.
D. The loopback addresses haven't been advertised, and the network command is missing on R4.

**Answer: B**
**Explanation:**
For an EIGRP neighbor to form, the following must match:
- Neighbors must be in the same subnet- K values- AS numbers- Authentication method and key
strings
Here, we see that R4 is configured for EIGRP AS 2, when it should be AS 1.

```
R4                                          R5
!                                           interface Ethernet0/2
interface Ethernet0/2                        no ip address
 no ip address                               shutdown
 shutdown                                   !
!                                           interface Ethernet0/3
interface Ethernet0/3                        no ip address
 no ip address                               shutdown
 shutdown                                   !
!                                           !
!                                           router eigrp 1
router eigrp 2                               network 10.5.5.5 0.0.0.0
 network 10.4.4.4 0.0.0.0                    network 10.5.5.55 0.0.0.0
 network 10.4.4.5 0.0.0.0                    network 10.10.10.0 0.0.0.255
 network 10.4.4.6 0.0.0.0                    network 192.168.123.0
 network 192.168.123.0                      !
!                                           ip forward-protocol nd
ip forward-protocol nd                      !
!                                           !
!                                           no ip http server
no ip http server                           no ip http secure-server
no ip http secure-server                    !
!                                           !
!                                           !
!                                           !
 --- More (18) ---                          control-plane
```

152. Hotspot Question

*Refer to the topology. Your company has connected the routers R1. R2. and R3 with serial links.*
*R2 and R3 are connected to the switches SW1 and SW2, respectively. SW1 and SW2 are also*
*connected to the routers R4 and R5.*
*The EIGRP routing protocol is configured.*
*You are required to troubleshoot and resolve the EIGRP issues between the various routers.*
*Use the appropriate show commands to troubleshoot the issues.*

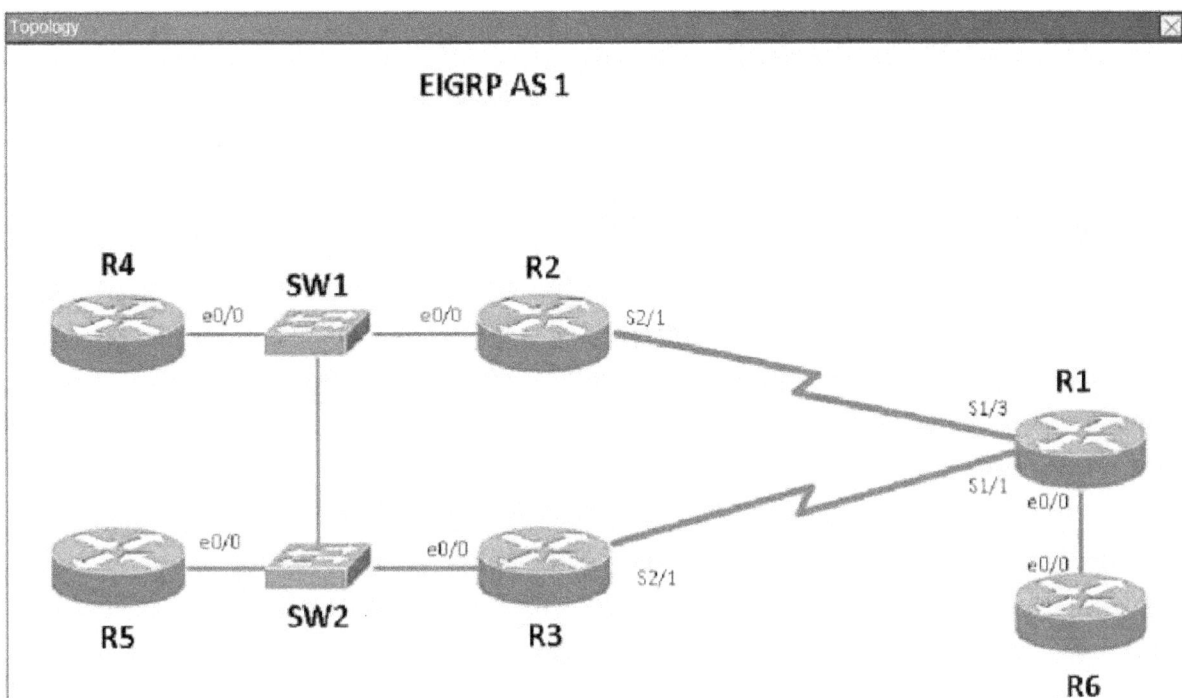

**Which path does traffic take from R1 to R5?**

A. The traffic goes through R2.
B. The traffic goes through R3.
C. The traffic is equally load-balanced over R2 and R3.
D. The traffic is unequally load-balanced over R2 and R3.

**Answer: A**
**Explanation:**
Using the "show ip int brief command" on R5 we can see the IP addresses assigned to this router.
Then, using the "show ip route" command on R1 we can see that to reach 10.5.5.5 and 10.5.5.55
the preferred path is via Serial 1/3, which we see from the diagram is the link to R2.

```
R1
Codes: L - local, C - connected, S - static, R - RIP, M - mobile, B -
       D - EIGRP, EX - EIGRP external, O - OSPF, IA - OSPF inter area
       N1 - OSPF NSSA external type 1, N2 - OSPF NSSA external type 2
       E1 - OSPF external type 1, E2 - OSPF external type 2
       i - IS-IS, su - IS-IS summary, L1 - IS-IS level-1, L2 - IS-IS
       ia - IS-IS inter area, * - candidate default, U - per-user sta
       o - ODR, P - periodic downloaded static route, H - NHRP, l - L
       + - replicated route, % - next hop override

Gateway of last resort is not set

      10.0.0.0/32 is subnetted, 5 subnets
C        10.1.1.1 is directly connected, Loopback0
D        10.2.2.2 [90/2297856] via 192.168.12.2, 00:37:12, Serial1/3
D        10.3.3.3 [90/2297856] via 192.168.13.3, 00:37:12, Serial1/1
D        10.5.5.5 [90/2323456] via 192.168.12.2, 00:37:12, Serial1/3
D        10.5.5.55 [90/2323456] via 192.168.12.2, 00:37:12, Serial1/3
      192.168.12.0/24 is variably subnetted, 2 subnets, 2 masks
C        192.168.12.0/24 is directly connected, Serial1/3
L        192.168.12.1/32 is directly connected, Serial1/3
      192.168.13.0/24 is variably subnetted, 2 subnets, 2 masks
C        192.168.13.0/24 is directly connected, Serial1/1
L        192.168.13.1/32 is directly connected, Serial1/1
      192.168.16.0/24 is variably subnetted, 2 subnets, 2 masks

R1#
```

```
R5
!
!
no ip http server
no ip http secure-server
!
!
!
control-plane
!
R5#show ip int brief
Interface       IP-Address      OK? Method Status                Protocol
Ethernet0/0     192.168.123.5   YES NVRAM  up                    up
Ethernet0/1     unassigned      YES NVRAM  administratively down down
Ethernet0/2     unassigned      YES NVRAM  administratively down down
Ethernet0/3     unassigned      YES NVRAM  administratively down down
Loopback0       10.5.5.5        YES NVRAM  up                    up
Loopback1       10.5.5.55       YES NVRAM  up                    up
R5#
```

R6

### 153. Hotspot Question

*Refer to the topology. Your company has connected the routers R1. R2. and R3 with serial links.*
*R2 and R3 are connected to the switches SW1 and SW2, respectively. SW1 and SW2 are also*
*connected to the routers R4 and R5.*
*The EIGRP routing protocol is configured.*
*You are required to troubleshoot and resolve the EIGRP issues between the various routers.*
*Use the appropriate show commands to troubleshoot the issues.*

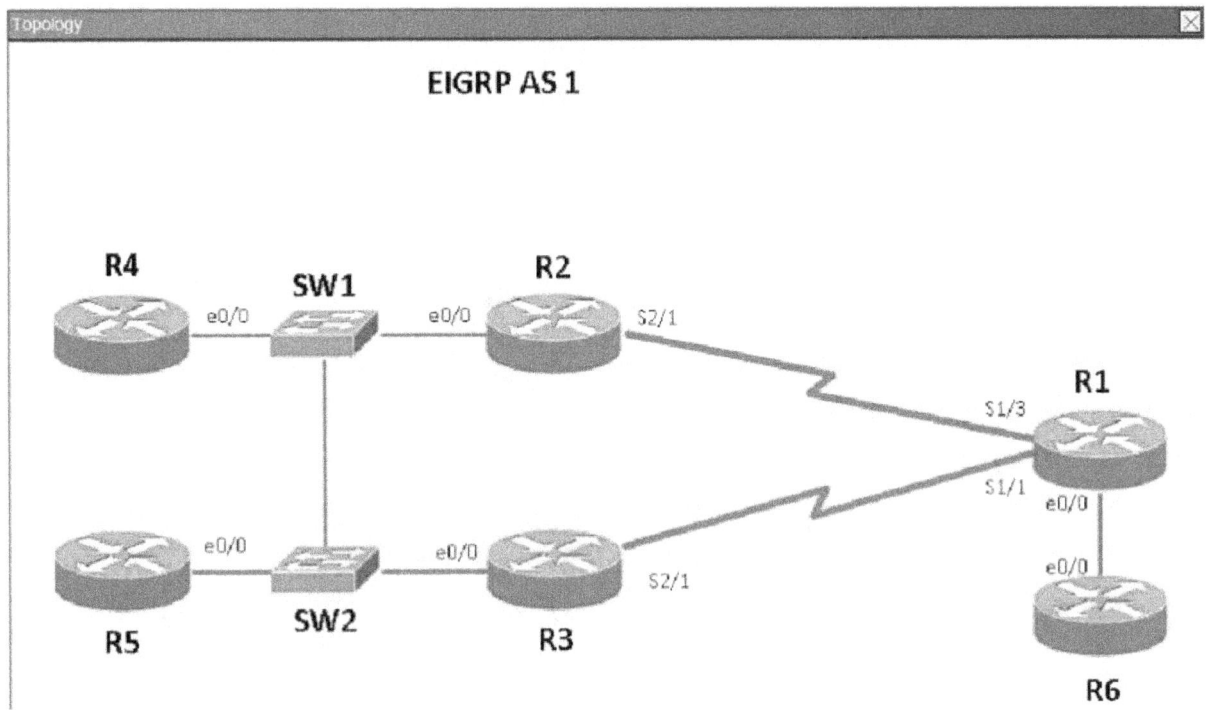

**Router R6 does not form an EIGRP neighbor relationship correctly with router R1. What is the cause for this misconfiguration?**

A. The K values mismatch.
B. The AS does not match.
C. The network command is missing.
D. The passive-interface command is enabled.

**Answer: C**
**Explanation:**
The link from R1 to R6 is shown below:

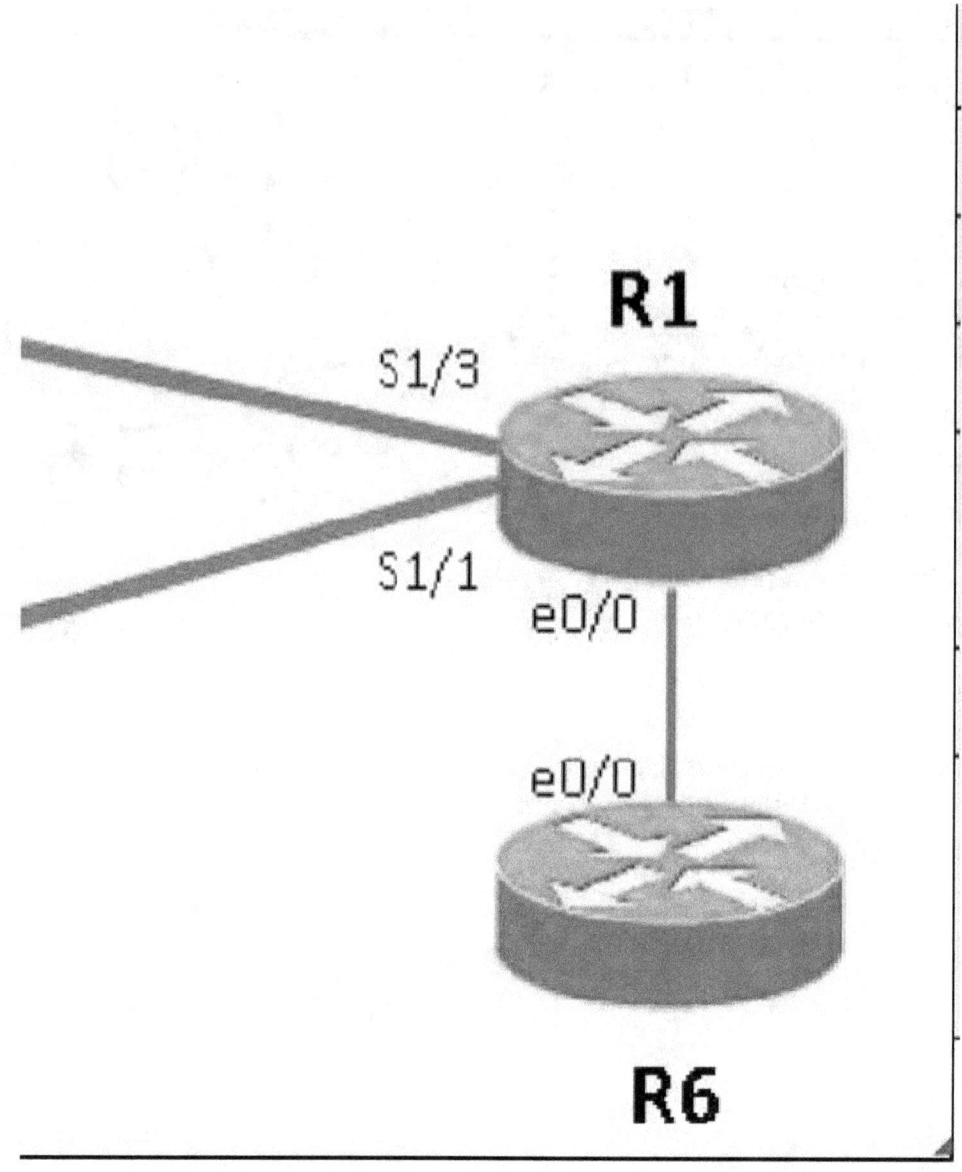

As you can see, they are both using e0/0. The IP addresses are in the 192.168.16.0 network:

| R1 | | | | R6 | | | |
|---|---|---|---|---|---|---|---|
| Interface | IP-Address | OK? Method | Status Protocol | R6# | | | |
| Ethernet0/0 | 192.168.16.1 | YES NVRAM | up | R6# | | | |
| Ethernet0/1 | unassigned | YES NVRAM | administratively down | R6#show ip int brief | | | |
| Ethernet0/2 | unassigned | YES NVRAM | administratively down | Interface | IP-Address | OK? Method | Status Protocol |
| Ethernet0/3 | unassigned | YES NVRAM | administratively down | Ethernet0/0 | 192.168.16.6 | YES NVRAM | up  up |
| Serial1/0 | unassigned | YES NVRAM | administratively down | Ethernet0/1 | unassigned | YES NVRAM | administratively down  down |
| Serial1/1 | 192.168.13.1 | YES NVRAM | up | Ethernet0/2 | unassigned | YES NVRAM | administratively down  down |
| Serial1/2 | unassigned | YES NVRAM | up | Ethernet0/3 | unassigned | YES NVRAM | administratively down  down |
| Serial1/3 | 192.168.12.1 | YES NVRAM | up | Serial1/0 | unassigned | YES NVRAM | administratively down  down |
| Serial2/0 | unassigned | YES NVRAM | administratively down | Serial1/1 | unassigned | YES NVRAM | up  down |
| Serial2/1 | unassigned | YES NVRAM | up | Serial1/2 | unassigned | YES NVRAM | administratively down  down |
| Serial2/2 | unassigned | YES NVRAM | administratively down | Serial1/3 | unassigned | YES NVRAM | administratively down  down |
| | | | | Loopback0 | 10.6.6.6 | YES NVRAM | up  up |
| R1# | | | | R6# | | | |

**But when we look at the EIGRP configuration, the "network 192.168.16.0" command is missing on R6.**

Study the following output taken on R1:

| R1 | R6 |
|---|---|
| ```
 shutdown
 serial restart-delay 0
!
interface Serial2/1
 no ip address
 serial restart-delay 0
!
interface Serial2/2
 no ip address
 shutdown
 serial restart-delay 0
!
interface Serial2/3
 no ip address
 shutdown
 serial restart-delay 0
!
!
router eigrp 1
 network 192.168.12.0
 network 192.168.13.0
 network 192.168.16.0
!
ip forward-protocol nd

R1#
``` | ```
 serial restart-delay 0
!
interface Serial1/1
 no ip address
 serial restart-delay 0
!
interface Serial1/2
 no ip address
 shutdown
 serial restart-delay 0
!
interface Serial1/3
 no ip address
 shutdown
 serial restart-delay 0
!
!
router eigrp 1
 network 10.6.6.6 0.0.0.0
!
ip forward-protocol nd
!
!
no ip http server

R6#
``` |

R1# Ping 10.5.5.55 source 10.1.1.1
Type escape sequence to abort.
Sending 5, 100-byte ICMP Echos to 10.5.5.55, timeout is 2 seconds:
Packet sent with a source address of 10.1.1.1

.......
Success rate is 0 percent (0/5)

**154. Hotspot Question**

Refer to the topology. Your company has connected the routers R1. R2. and R3 with serial links.
R2 and R3 are connected to the switches SW1 and SW2, respectively. SW1 and SW2 are also
connected to the routers R4 and R5.
The EIGRP routing protocol is configured.
You are required to troubleshoot and resolve the EIGRP issues between the various routers. Use the appropriate show commands to troubleshoot the issues.

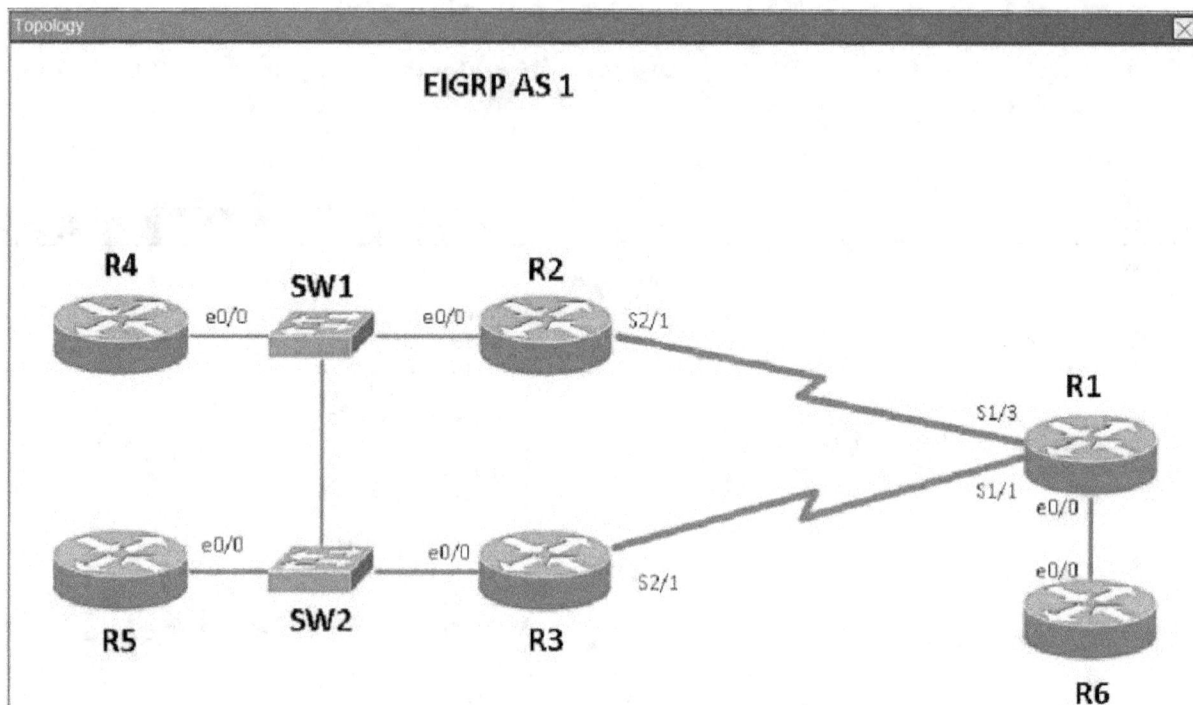

**Why are the pings failing?**

A. The network statement is missing on R5.
B. The loopback interface is shut down on R5.
C. The network statement is missing on R1.
D. The IP address that is configured on the Lo1 interface on R5 is incorrect.

**Answer: C**
**Explanation:**
R5 does not have a route to the 10.1.1.1 network, which is the loopback0 IP address of R1. When looking at the EIGRP configuration on R1, we see that the 10.1.1.1 network statement is missing on R1.

```
R1
 no ip address
 serial restart-delay 0
!
interface Serial2/2
 no ip address
 shutdown
 serial restart-delay 0
!
interface Serial2/3
 no ip address
 shutdown
 serial restart-delay 0
!
!
router eigrp 1
 network 192.168.12.0
 network 192.168.13.0
 network 192.168.16.0
!
ip forward-protocol nd
!
!
no ip http server
no ip http secure-server

R1#
```

155. What is a valid HSRP virtual MAC address?

A. 0000.5E00.01A3
B. 0007.B400.AE01
C. 0000.0C07.AC15
D. 0007.5E00.B301

**Answer: C**
**Explanation:**
With HSRP, two or more devices support a virtual router with a fictitious MAC address and unique IP address. There are two version of HSRP.
+ With HSRP version 1, the virtual router's MAC address is 0000.0c07.ACxx , in which xx is the HSRP group.
+ With HSRP version 2, the virtual MAC address if 0000.0C9F.Fxxx, in which xxx is the HSRP group.
Note: Another case is HSRP for IPv6, in which the MAC address range from 0005.73A0.0000 through 0005.73A0.0FFF.

### 156. In GLBP, which router will respond to client ARP requests?

A. The active virtual gateway will reply with one of four possible virtual MAC addresses.
B. All GLBP member routers will reply in round-robin fashion.
C. The active virtual gateway will reply with its own hardware MAC address.
D. The GLBP member routers will reply with one of four possible burned in hardware addresses.

**Answer: A**
**Explanation:**
One disadvantage of HSRP and VRRP is that only one router is in use, other routers must wait for the primary to fail because they can be used. However, Gateway Load Balancing Protocol (GLBP) can use of up to four routers simultaneously. In GLBP, there is still only one virtual IP address but each router has a different virtual MAC address. First a GLBP group must elect an Active Virtual Gateway (AVG). The AVG is responsible for replying ARP requests from hosts/clients. It replies with different virtual MAC addresses that correspond to different routers (known as Active Virtual Forwarders - AVFs) so that clients can send traffic to different routers in that GLBP group (load sharing).

### 157. Which statement describes VRRP object tracking?

A. It monitors traffic flow and link utilization.
B. It ensures the best VRRP router is the virtual router master for the group.
C. It causes traffic to dynamically move to higher bandwidth links.
D. It thwarts man-in-the-middle attacks.

**Answer:**
**Explanation:**
Object tracking is the process of tracking the state of a configured object and uses that state to
determine the priority of the VRRP router in a VRRP group

### 158. What is a global command?

A. a command that is set once and affects the entire router
B. a command that is implemented in all foreign and domestic IOS versions
C. a command that is universal in application and supports all protocols
D. a command that is available in every release of IOS, regardless of the version or deployment status
E. a command that can be entered in any configuration mode

**Answer: A**
**Explanation:**
When you enter global configuration mode and enter a command, it is applied to the running
configuration file that is currently running in ram. The configuration of a global command affects the
entire router. An example of a global command is one used for the hostname of the router.

159. An administrator is unsuccessful in adding VLAN 50 to a switch. While troubleshooting the problem, the administrator views the output of the show vtp status command, which is displayed in the graphic. What commands must be issued on this switch to add VLAN 50 to the database? (Choose two.)

```
Switch# show vtp status

VTP Version                        : 2
Configuration Revision             : 7
Maximum VLANs supported local      : 68
Number of existing VLANs           : 8
VTP Operating Mode                 : Client
VTP Domain Name                    : corp
VTP Pruning Mode                   : Disabled
VTP V2 Mode                        : Disabled
VTP Traps Generation               : Disabled
MD5 digest                         : 0x22 0xF3 0x1A
Configuration last modified by 172.18.22.15 at 5-28-03 11:53:20
```

A. Switch(config-if)# switchport access vlan 50
B. Switch(vlan)# vtp server
C. Switch(config)# config-revision 20
D. Switch(config)# vlan 50 name Tech
E. Switch(vlan)# vlan 50
F. Switch(vlan)# switchport trunk vlan 50

Answer: BE

160. Which of the following IP addresses fall into the CIDR block of 115.64.4.0/22? (Choose three.)

A. 115.64.8.32
B. 115.64.7.64
C. 115.64.6.255
D. 115.64.3.255
E. 115.64.5.128
F. 115.64.12.128

Answer: BCE

161. Which of the following are types of flow control? (Choose three.)

A. buffering
B. cut-through
C. windowing
D. congestion avoidance
E. load balancing

Answer: ACD

162. Refer to the exhibit. After a RIP route is marked invalid on Router_1, how much time will elapse before that route is removed from the routing table?

```
Router_1# show ip protocols
Routing Protocol is "rip"
  Sending updates every 30 seconds, next due in 8 seconds
  Invalid after 180 seconds, hold down 180, flushed after 240
  Outgoing update filter list for all interfaces is not set
  Incoming update filter list for all interfaces is not set
  <output omitted>

Router_1#
```

A. 30 seconds
B. 60 seconds
C. 90 seconds
D. 180 seconds
E. 240 seconds

Answer: E

105. Refer to the exhibit. A network associate has configured the internetwork that is shown in the exhibit, but has failed to configure routing properly.

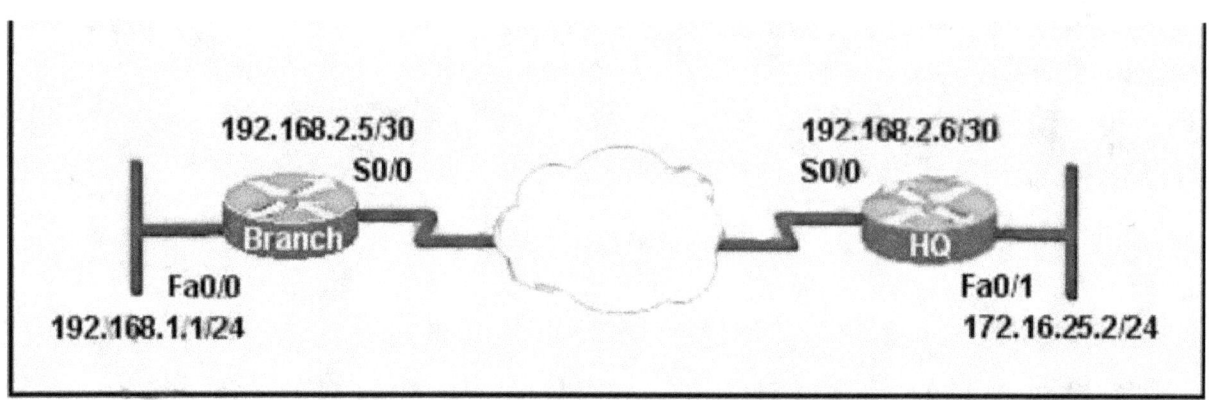

Which configuration will allow the hosts on the Branch LAN to access resources on the HQ LANM with the least impact on router processing and WAN bandwidth?

A. HQ(config)# ip route 192.168.1.0 255.255.255.0 192.168.2.5
Branch(config)# ip route 172.16.25.0 255.255.255.0 192.168.2.6

B. HQ(config)# router rip
HQ(config-router)# network 192.168.2.0

HQ(config-router)# network 172.16.0.0
Branch(config)# router rip
Branch(config-router)# network 192.168.1.0
Branch(config-router)# network 192.168.2.0

C. HQ(config)# router eigrp 56
HQ(config-router)# network 192.168.2.4
HQ(config-router)# network 172.16.25.0
Branch(config)# router eigrp 56
Branch(config-router)# network 192.168.1.0
Branch(config-router)# network 192.168.2.4

D. HQ(config)# router ospf 1
HQ(config-router)# network 192.168.2.4 0.0.0.3 area 0
HQ(config-router)# network 172.16.25.0 0.0.0.255 area 0
Branch(config)# router ospf 1
Branch(config-router)# network 192.168.1.0 0.0.0.255 area 0

Answer: A

163. Which additional configuration step is necessary in order to connect to an access point that has SSID broadcasting disabled?

A. Set the SSID value in the client software to public.
B. Configure open authentication on the AP and the client.
C. Set the SSID value on the client to the SSID configured on the AP.
D. Configured MAC address filtering to permit the client to connect to the AP.

Answer: D

164. What is one reason that WPA encryption is preferred over WEP?

A. A WPA key is longer and requires more special characters than the WEP key.
B. The access point and the client are manually configured with different WPA key values.
C. WPA key values remain the same until the client configuration is changed.
D. The values of WPA keys can change dynamically while the system is used.

Answer: D

165. All WAN links inside the ABC University network use PPP with CHAP for authentication security. Which command will display the CHAP authentication process as it occur between two routers in the network?

A. show chap authentication
B. show interface serial0
C. debug ppp authentication
D. debug chap authentication
E. show ppp authentication chap

Answer: C

166. Refer to the exhibit. The network is converged. After link-state advertisements are received from Router_A, what information will Router_E contain in its routing table for the subnets 208.149.23.64 and 208.149.23.96?

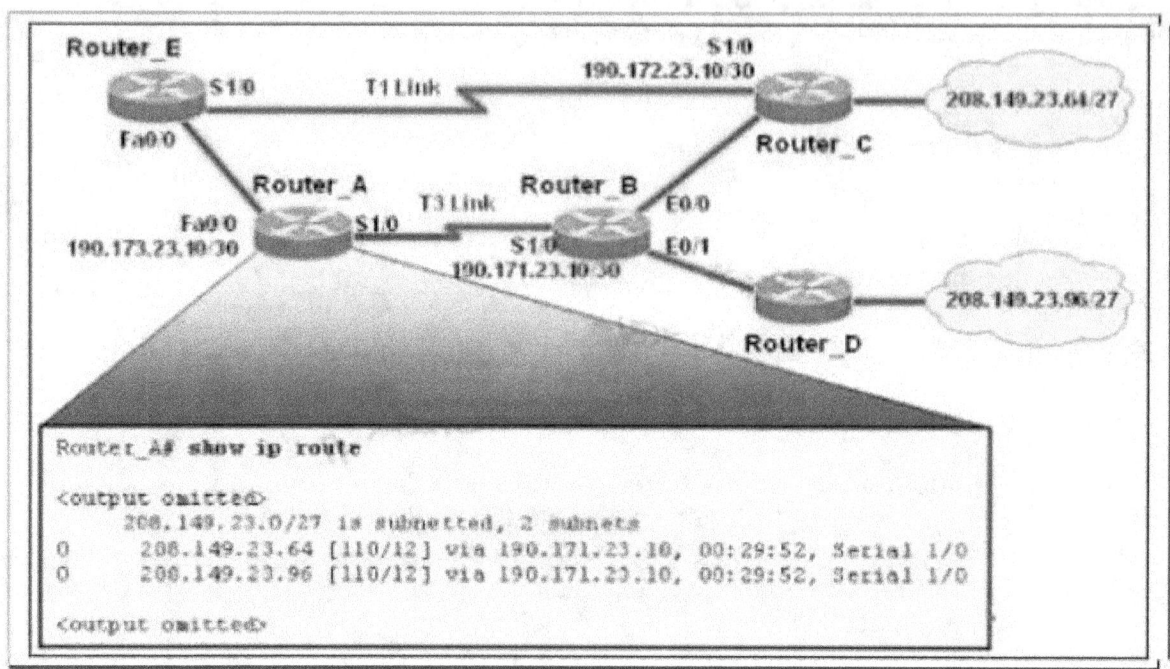

A. 208.149.23.64[110/13] via 190.173.23.10, 00:00:00:07, FastEthernet0/0
208.149.23.96[110/13] via 190.173.23.10, 00:00:00:16, FastEthernet0/0

B. 208.149.23.64[110/1] via 190.173.23.10, 00:00:00:07, Serial1/0
208.149.23.96[110/3] via 190.173.23.10, 00:00:00:16, FastEthernet0/0

C. 208.149.23.64[110/13] via 190.173.23.10, 00:00:00:07, Serial1/0
208.149.23.96[110/13] via 190.173.23.10, 00:00:00:16, Serial1/0
208.149.23.96[110/13] via 190.173.23.10, 00:00:00:16, FastEthernet0/0

D. 208.149.23.64[110/13] via 190.173.23.10, 00:00:00:07, Serial1/0
208.149.23.96[110/13] via 190.173.23.10, 00:00:00:16, Serial1/0

Answer: A

167. What are two characteristics of SSH? (Choose two.)

A. most common remote-access method
B. unsecured
C. encrypted
D. uses port 22
E. operates at the transport layer

Answer: DE

168. Refer to the exhibit. The access list has been configured on the S0/0 interface of router RTB in the outbound direction. Which two packets, if routed to the interface, will be denied? (Choose two.) access-list 101 deny tcp 192.168.15.32 0.0.0.15 any eq telnet access-list 101 permit ip any any

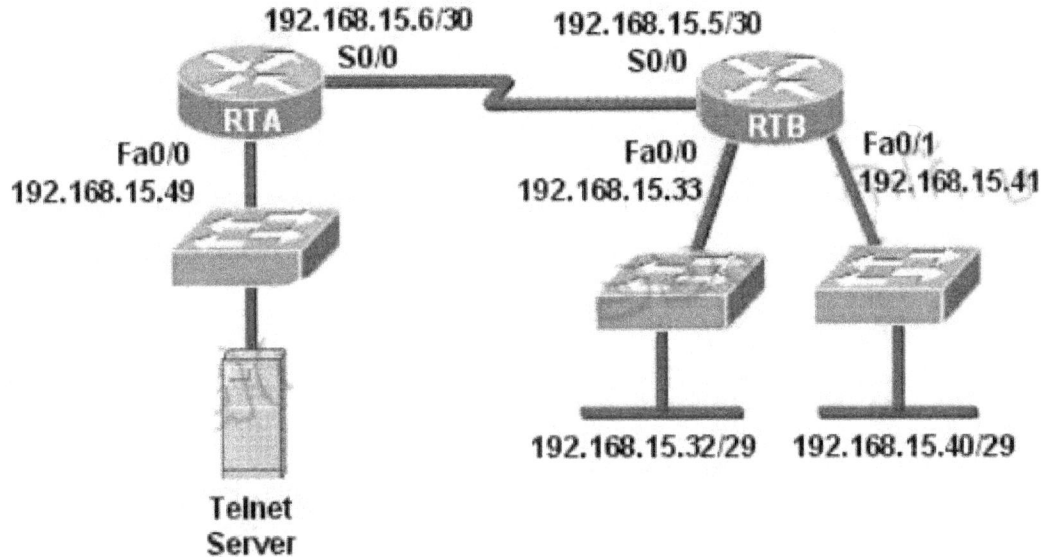

A. source ip address: 192.168.15.5; destination port: 21
B. source ip address:, 192.168.15.37 destination port: 21
C. source ip address:, 192.168.15.41 destination port: 21
D. source ip address:, 192.168.15.36 destination port: 23
E. source ip address: 192.168.15.46; destination port: 23
F. source ip address:, 192.168.15.49 destination port: 23

Answer: DE

169. Refer to the graphic. It has been decided that Workstation 1 should be denied access to Server1. Which of the following commands are required to prevent only Workstation 1 from accessing Server1 while allowing all other traffic to flow normally? (Choose two.)

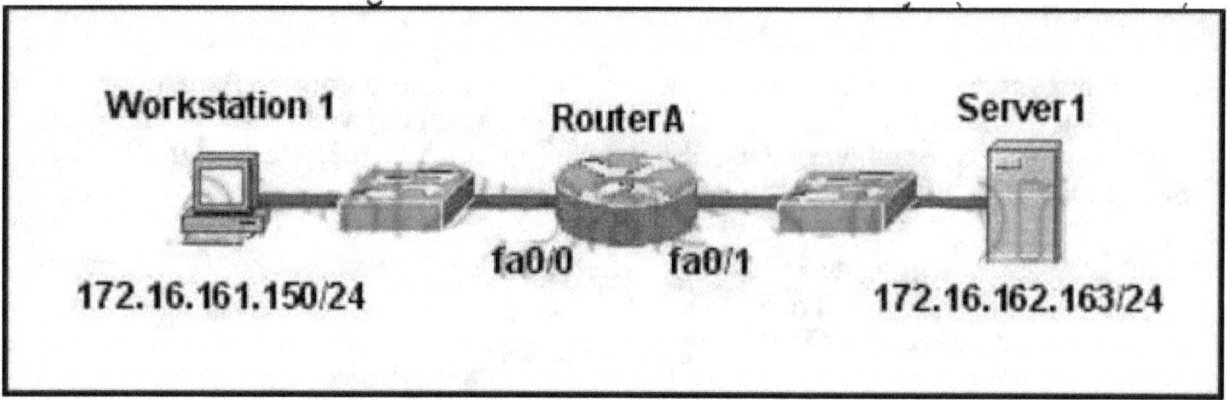

A. RouterA(config)# interface fa0/0
RouterA(config-if)# ip access-group 101 out

B. RouterA(config)# interface fa0/0
RouterA(config-if)# ip access-group 101 in

C. RouterA(config)# access-list 101 deny ip host 172.16.161.150 host 172.16.162.163
RouterA(config)# access-list 101 permit ip any any

D. RouterA(config)# access-list 101 deny ip 172.16.161.150 0.0.0.255 172.16.162.163 0.0.0.0
RouterA(config)# access-list 101 permit ip any any

Answer: BC

**170.** An access list was written with the four statements shown in the graphic. Which single access list statement will combine all four of these statements into a single statement that will have exactly the same effect? _____

```
access-list 10 permit 172.29.16.0 0.0.0.255
access-list 10 permit 172.29.17.0 0.0.0.255
access-list 10 permit 172.29.18.0 0.0.0.255
access-list 10 permit 172.29.19.0 0.0.0.255
```

A. access-list 10 permit 172.29.16.0 0.0.0.255
B. access-list 10 permit 172.29.16.0 0.0.1.255
C. access-list 10 permit 172.29.16.0 0.0.3.255
D. access-list 10 permit 172.29.16.0 0.0.15.255
E. access-list 10 permit 172.29.0.0 0.0.255.255

Answer: C

**171.** A network administrator wants to add a line to an access list that will block only Telnet access by the hosts on subnet 192.168.1.128/28 to the server at 192.168.1.5. What command should be issued to accomplish this task?

A. access-list 101 deny tcp 192.168.1.128 0.0.0.15 192.168.1.5 0.0.0.0 eq 23
access-list 101 permit ip any any

B. access-list 101 deny tcp 192.168.1.128 0.0.0.240 192.168.1.5 0.0.0.0 eq 23
access-list 101 permit ip any any

C. access-list 1 deny tcp 192.168.1.128 0.0.0.255 192.168.1.5 0.0.0.0 eq 21
access-list 1 permit ip any any

D. access-list 1 deny tcp 192.168.1.128 0.0.0.15 host 192.168.1.5 eq 23
access-list 1 permit ip any any

Answer: A

172. As a network administrator, you have been instructed to prevent all traffic originating on the LAN from entering the R2 router. Which the following command would implement the access list on the interface of the R2 router?

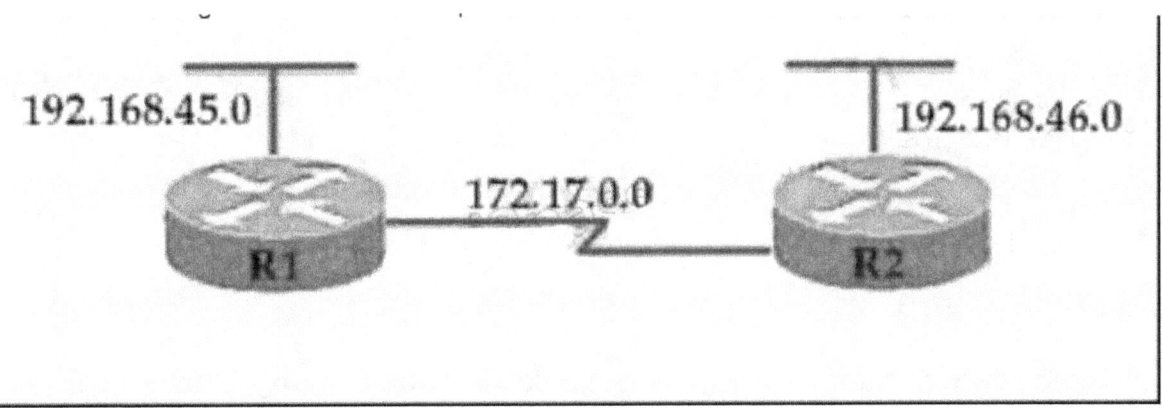

A. access-list 101 in
B. access-list 101 out
C. ip access-group 101 in
D. ip access-group 101 out

Answer: C

173. The access control list shown in the graphic has been applied to the Ethernet interface of router R1 using the ip access-group 101 in command.
Which of the following Telnet sessions will be blocked by this ACL? (Choose two.)

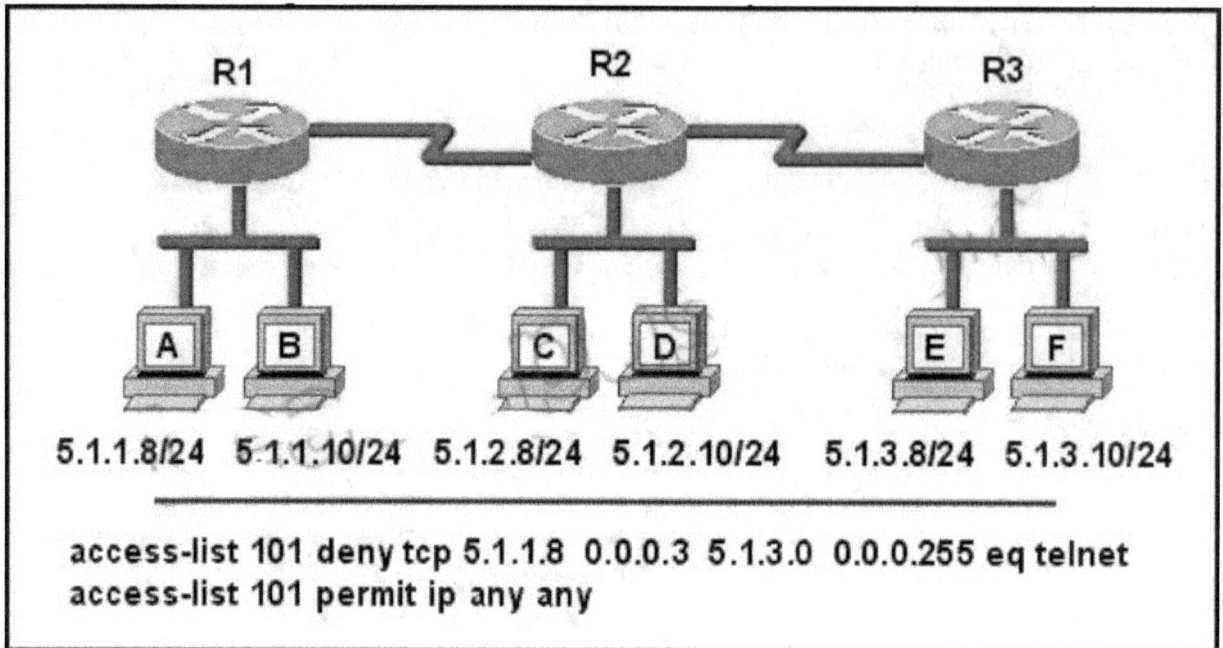

A. from host A to host 5.1.1.10
B. from host A to host 5.1.3.10
C. from host B to host 5.1.2.10
D. from host B to host 5.1.3.8
E. from host C to host 5.1.3.10
F. from host F to host 5.1.1.10

Answer: BD

174. The following access list below was applied outbound on the E0 interface connected to the 192.169.1.8/29 LAN: access-list 135 deny tcp 192.169.1.8 0.0.0.7 eq 20 any access-list 135 deny tcp 192.169.1.8 0.0.0.7 eq 21 any How will the above access lists affect traffic?

A. FTP traffic from 192.169.1.22 will be denied
B. No traffic, except for FTP traffic will be allowed to exit E0
C. FTP traffic from 192.169.1.9 to any host will be denied
D. All traffic exiting E0 will be denied
E. All FTP traffic to network 192.169.1.9/29 will be denied

Answer: D

175. The following configuration line was added to router R1 Access-list 101 permit ip 10.25.30.0 0.0.0.255 any. What is the effect of this access list configuration?

A. ermit all packets matching the first three octets of the source address to all destinations
B. permit all packet matching the last octet of the destination address and accept all source addresses

C. permit all packet matching the host bits in the source address to all destinations
D. permit all packet from the third subnet of the network address to all destinations

Answer: A

**176. A default Frame Relay WAN is classified as what type of physical network?**

A. point-to-point
B. broadcast multi-access
C. nonbroadcast multi-access
D. nonbroadcast multipoint
E. broadcast point-to-multipoint

Answer: C

**177. Which of the following are key characteristics of PPP? (Choose three.)**

A. can be used over analog circuits
B. maps Layer 2 to Layer 3 address
C. encapsulates several routed protocols
D. supports IP only
E. provides error correction

Answer: ACE

**178. How should a router that is being used in a Frame Relay network be configured to avoid split horizon issues from preventing routing updates?**

A. Configure a separate sub-interface for each PVC with a unique DLCI and subnet assigned to the
sub-interface
B. Configure each Frame Relay circuit as a point-to-point line to support multicast and broadcast traffic
C. Configure many sub-interfaces on the same subnet
D. Configure a single sub-interface to establish multiple PVC connections to multiple remote router interfaces

Answer: A

**179. The Frame Relay network in the diagram is not functioning properly. What is the cause of the problem?**

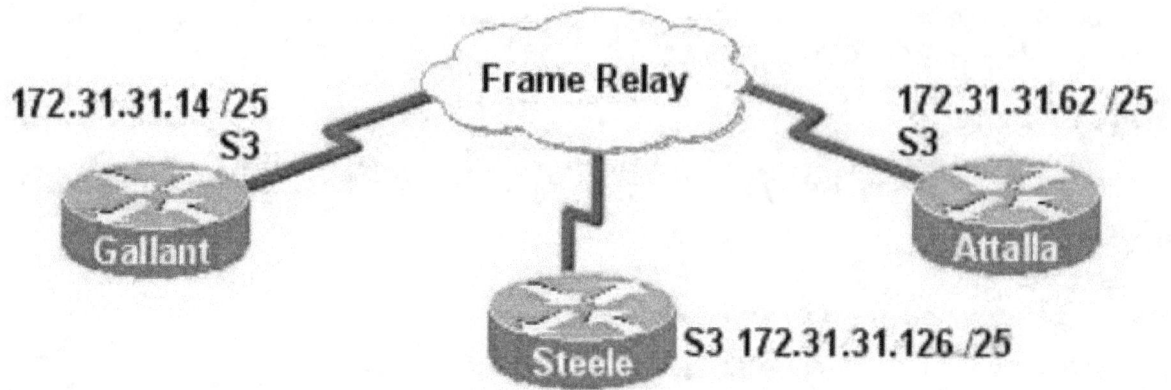

A. The Gallant router has the wrong LMI type configured
B. Inverse ARP is providing the wrong PVC information to the Gallant router
C. The S3 interface of the Steele router has been configured with the frame-relay encapsulation ietf
command
D. The frame-relay map statement in the Attalla router for the PVC to Steele is not correct
E. The IP address on the serial interface of the Attalla router is configured incorrectly

Answer: D

180. As a CCNA candidate, you must have a firm understanding of the IPv6 address structure. Refer to IPv6 address, could you tell me how many bits are included in each filed?

A. 24
B. 4
C. 3
D. 16

Answer: D

181. Refer to the exhibit. How many broadcast domains exist in the exhibited topology?

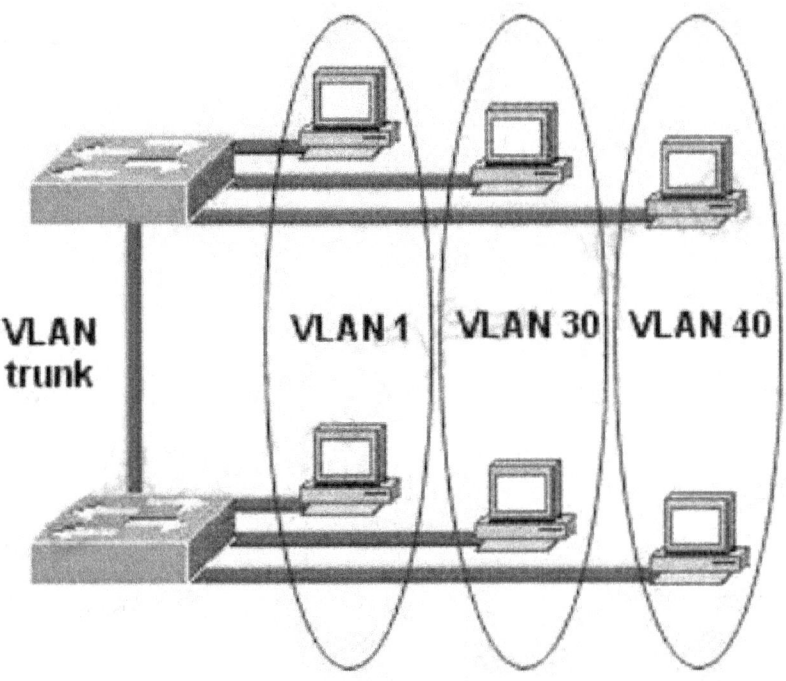

A. one
B. two
C. three
D. four
E. five
F. six

Answer: C

182. Refer to the exhibit. The network administrator has created a new VLAN on Switch1 and added host C and host D. The administrator has properly configured switch interfaces FastEthernet0/13 throughFastEthernet0/14 to be members of the new VLAN. However, after the network administrator completed the configuration, host A could communicate with host B, but host A could not communicate with host C or host D. Which commands are required to resolve this problem?

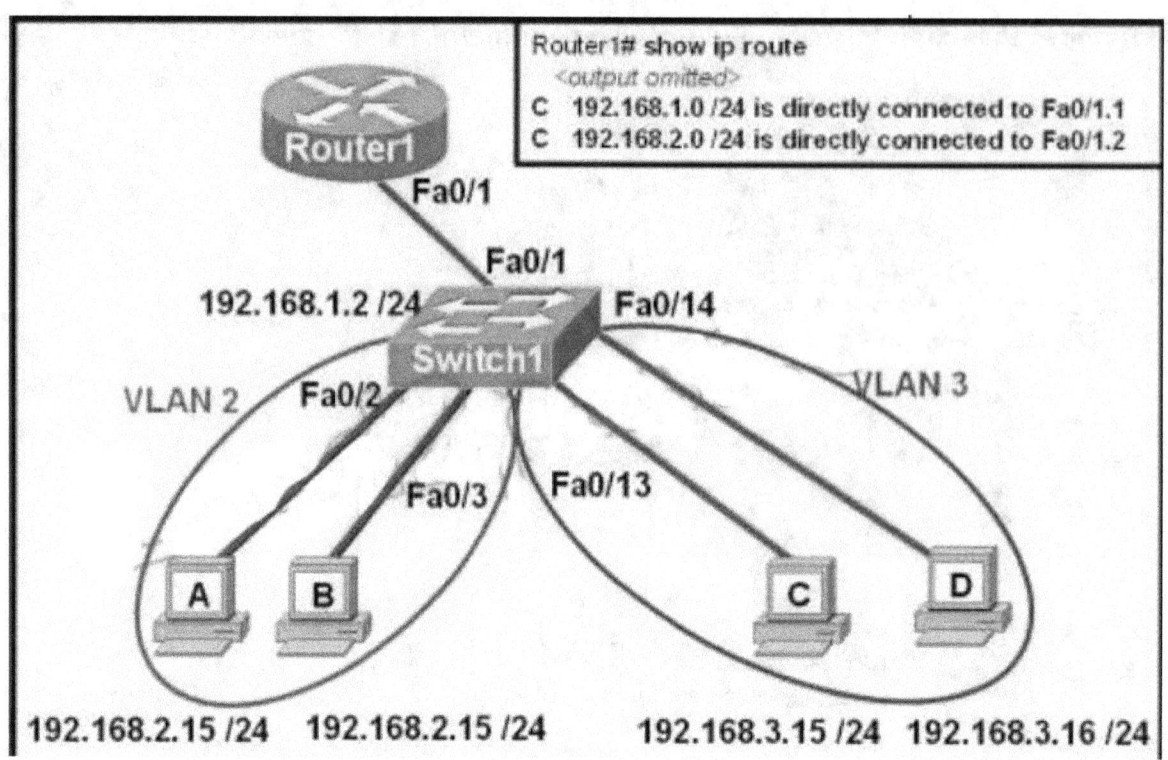

A. Router(config)# interface fastethernet 0/1.3
Router(config-if)# encapsulation dot1q 3
Router(config-if)# ip address 192.168.3.1 255.255.255.0

B. Router(config)# router rip
Router(config-router)# network 192.168.1.0
Router(config-router)# network 192.168.2.0
Router(config-router)# network192.168.3.0

C. Switch1# vlan database
Switch1(vlan)# vtp v2-mode
Switch1(vlan)# vtp domain cisco
Switch1(vlan)# vtp server

D. Switch1(config)# interface fastethernet 0/1
Switch1(config-if)# switchport mode trunk
Switch1(config-if)# switchport trunk encapsulation isl

Answer: A

183. On a network of one department, there are four PCs connected to a switch, as shown in the following figure: After the Switch1 restarts. Host A ( the host on the left ) sends the first frame to Host C (the host on the right). What the first thing should the switch do?

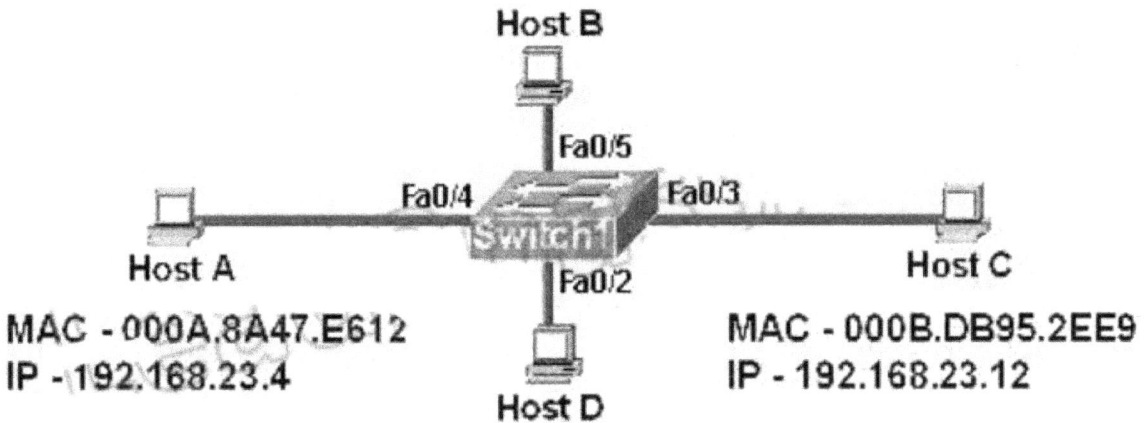

A. Switch1 will add 192.168.23.12 to the switching table.
B. Switch1 will add 192.168.23.4 to the switching table.
C. Switch1 will add 000A.8A47.E612 to the switching table.
D. None of the above

Answer: C

184. Refer to the exhibit. The network administrator is in a campus building distant from Building B. WANRouter is hosting a newly installed WAN link on interface S0/0. The new link is not functioning and the administrator needs to determine if the correct cable has been attached to the S0/0 interface. How can the administrator accurately verify the correct cable type on S0/0 in the most efficient manner?

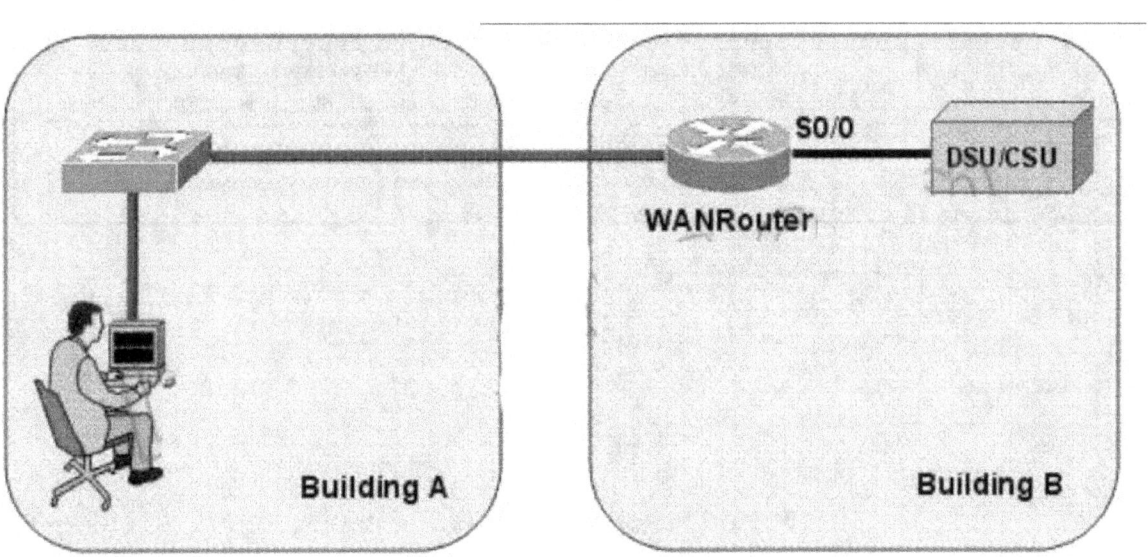

A. Telnet to WANRouter and execute the command show interfaces S0/0
B. Telnet to WANRouter and execute the command show processes S0/0
C. Telnet to WANRouter and execute the command show running-configuration
D. Telnet to WANRouter and execute the command show controller S0/0
E. Physically examine the cable between WANRouter S0/0 and the DCE.
F. Establish a console session on WANRouter and execute the command show interfaces S0/0

Answer: D

185. While troubleshooting a connectivity issue from a PC you obtain the following information:
Local PC IP address: 10.0.0.35/24
Default Gateway: 10.0.0.1
Remote Sever: 10.5.75.250/24
You then conduct the following tests from the local PC:
Ping 127.0.0.1 - Successful
Ping 10.0.0.35 - Successful
Ping 10.0.0.1 - Unsuccessful
Ping 10.5.75.250 – Unsuccessful

What is the underlying cause of this problem?

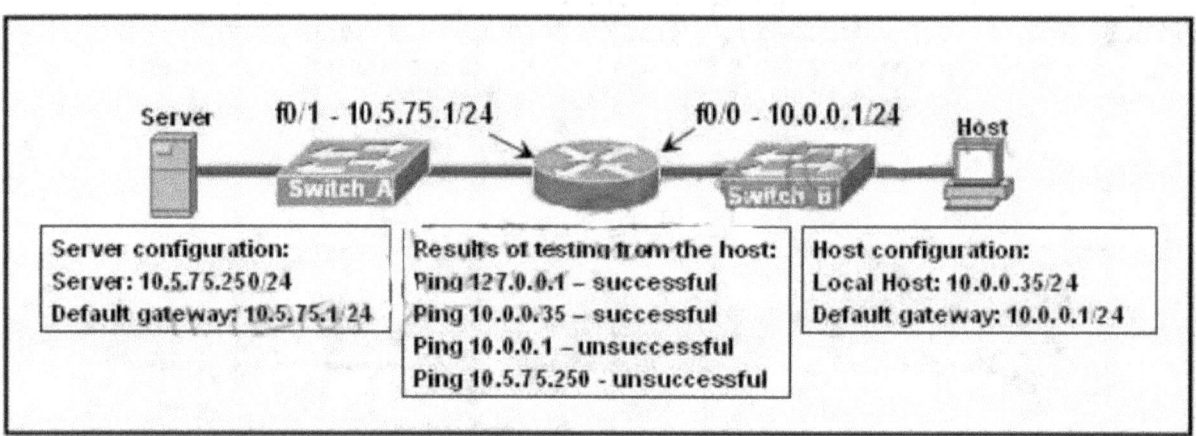

A. A remote physical layer problem exists.
B. The host NIC is not functioning.
C. TCP/IP has not been correctly installed on the host.
D. A local physical layer problem exists.

Answer: D

186. A network administrator is troubleshooting the OSPF configuration of routers R1 and R2. The routers cannot establish an adjacency relationship on their common Ethernet link. The graphic shows the output of the show ip ospf interface e0 command for routers R1 and R2.

```
R1:    Ethernet0 is up, line protocol is up
       Internet address 192.168.1.2/24, Area 0
       Process ID 1, Router ID 192.168.31.33, Network Type BROADCAST, Cost: 10
       Transmit Delay is 1 sec, State DR, Priority 1
       Designated Router (ID) 192.168.31.33, Interface address 192.168.1.2
       No backup designated router on this network
       Timer intervals configured, Hello 5, Dead 20, Wait 20, Retransmit 5

R2:    Ethernet0 is up, line protocol is up
       Internet address 192.168.1.1/24, Area 0
       Process ID 2, Router ID 192.168.31.11, Network Type BROADCAST, Cost: 10
       Transmit Delay is 1 sec, State DR, Priority 1
       Designated Router (ID) 192.168.31.11, Interface address 192.168.1.1
       No backup designated router on this network
       Timer intervals configured, Hello 10, Dead 40, Wait 40, Retransmit 5
```

Based on the information in the graphic, what is the cause of this problem?

A. The OSPF area is not configured properly.
B. The priority on R1 should be set higher.
C. The cost on R1 should be set higher.
D. The hello and dead timers are not configured properly.
E. A backup designated router needs to be added to the network.
F. The OSPF process ID numbers must match.

Answer: D

187. This graphic shows the results of an attempt to open a Telnet connection to router ACCESS1 from router Remote27.

```
Remote27#
Remote27#telnet access1
Trying ACCESS1 (10.0.0.1)... Open


Password required, but none set

[Connection to access1 closed by foreign host]
Remote27#
```

Which of the following command sequences will correct this problem?

A. ACCESS1(config)# line console 0
ACCESS1(config-line)# password cisco

B. Remote27(config)# line console 0
Remote27(config-line)# login
Remote27(config-line)# password cisco

C. ACCESS1(config)# line vty 0 4
ACCESS1(config-line)# login
ACCESS1(config-line)# password cisco

D. Remote27(config)# line vty 0 4
Remote27(config-line)# login
Remote27(config-line)# password cisco

E. ACCESS1(config)# enable password cisco

F. Remote27(config)# enable password cisco

Answer: C

188. When upgrading the IOS image, the network administrator receives the exhibited error message.

```
Router1#copy tftp flash
Address or name of remote host[ ]? 192.168.1.5
Source filename[ ]? c2600-js-1-121-3.bin
Destination filename [ c2600-js-1-121-3.bin
Accessing tftp://192.168.1.5 /c2600-js-1-121-3.bin...
%Error opening tftp://192.168.1.5 /CCC (Timed out)
```

What could be the cause of this error?

A. The new IOS image is too large for the router flash memory.
B. The TFTP server is unreachable from the router.
C. The new IOS image is not correct for this router platform.
D. The IOS image on the TFTP server is corrupt.
E. There is not enough disk space on the TFTP server for the IOS image.

Answer: B

189. Refer to the exhibit, Host A pings interface S0/0 on router 3, what is the TTL value for that ping?

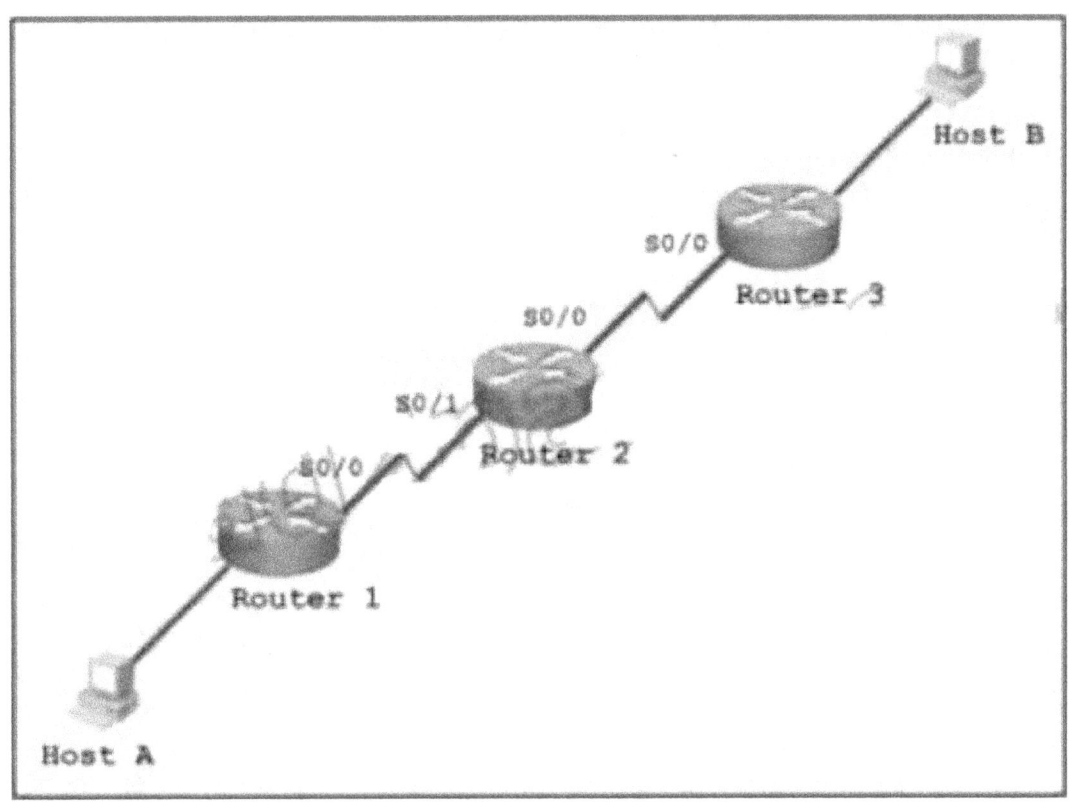

A. 253
B. 252
C. 255
D. 254

Answer: A

190. Which statement is true, as relates to classful or classless routing?

A. Automatic summarization at classful boundries can cause problems on discontinuous subnets
B. EIGRP and OSPF are classful routing protocols and summarize routes by default
C. RIPv1 and OSPF are classless routing protocols
D. Classful routing protocols send the subnet mask in routing updates

Answer: A

191. Refer to the exhibit. Why does the telnet connecting fail when a host attempts to connect a remote router?

```
Router-1#telnet 10.3.3.1
Trying 10.3.3.1 ... Open
Password required, but none set
[Connection to 10.3.3.1 clossed by foreign hostl]
```

A. No password was set for tty lines
B. No password was set for aux lines
C. No password was set for vty lines
D. No password was set for cty lines

Answer: C

**192. Which name describes an IPV6 host-enable tunneling technique that uses IPV4 UDP,does not require dedicated gateway tunnels,and can pass through existing IPV4 NAT gateways?**

A. dual stack
B. dynamic
C. Teredo
D. Manual 6to4

Answer: C

**193. Which pairing reflects a correct protocol-and-metric relationship?**

A. OSPF and mumber of hops and reliability
B. EIGRP and link cost
C. IS-IS and delay and reliability
D. RIPv2 and number of hops

Answer: D

**194. Refer to the exhibit, The VLAN configuration of S1 is not being in this VTP enabled environment. The VTP and uplink port configurations for each switch are displayed. Which two command sets, if issued, resolve this failure and allow VTP to operate as expected?(choose two)**

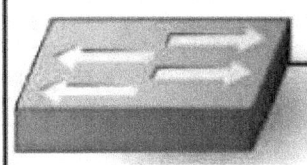
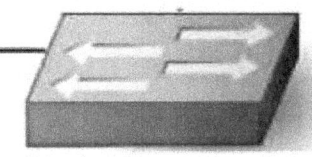

```
                    Fa0/24          Fa0/24
    S1                                        S2

S1#show running-config | include vtp
vtp mode transparent
vtp domain cisco
vtp password cisco

S1#show running-config interface Fa 0/24
interface FastEthernet0/24
   switchport mode access
   no ip address

S2#show running-config | include vtp
vtp mode server
vtp domain cisco
vtp password cisco

S2#show running-config interface Fa 0/24
interface FastEthernet0/24
   switchport mode dynamic auto
   no ip address
```

A. S2(config)#vtp mode transparent

B. S1(config)#vtp mode client

C. S2(config)#interface f0/24
S2(config-if)#switchport mode access
S2(config-if)#end

D. S2(config)#vtp mode client

E. S1(config)#interface f0/24
S1(config-if)#switchport mode trunk
S1(config-if)#end

**Answer: BE**

**195. How are VTP advertisements delivered to switches across the network?**

A. anycast frames
B. multicast frames
C. broadcast frames
D. unicast frames

Answer: B

196. Refer to the exhibit. What could be possible causes for the "Serial0/0 is down" interface status?
(Choose two.)

```
Router1# show interfaces serial 0/0

Serial0/0 is down, line protocol is down
   Hardware is MK5025
   Serial Internet address is 10.1.1.2/24
   MTU 1500 bytes, BW 1544 Kbits. DLY 20000 usec, rely 255/255 load 9/255
   Encapsulation PPP, loopback not set, keepalive set (10 sec)
```

A. A Layer 1 problem exists.
B. The bandwidth is set too low.
C. A protocol mismatch exists.
D. An incorrect cable is being used.
E. There is an incorrect IP address on the Serial 0/0 interface.

Answer: AD

197. Refer to the exhibit. Which two statements are true about the loopback address that is configured on RouterB? (Choose two.)

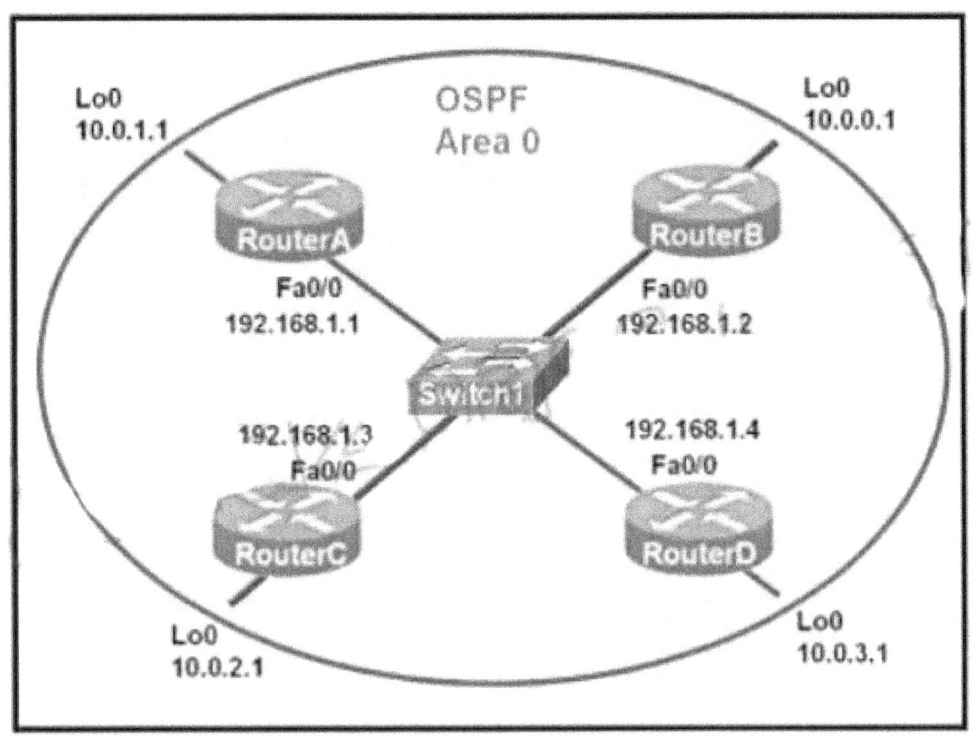

A. It ensures that data will be forwarded by RouterB.
B. It provides stability for the OSPF process on RouterB.
C. It specifies that the router ID for RouterB should be 10.0.0.1.
D. It decreases the metric for routes that are advertised from RouterB.
E. It indicates that RouterB should be elected the DR for the LAN.

Answer: BC

198. A network administrator is explaining VTP configuration to a new technician. What should the network administrator tell the new technician about VTP configuration? (Choose three.)

A. A switch in the VTP client mode cannot update its local VLAN database.

B. A trunk link must be configured between the switches to forward VTP updates.

C. A switch in the VTP server mode can update a switch in the VTP transparent mode.

D. A switch in the VTP transparent mode will forward updates that it receives to other switches.

E. A switch in the VTP server mode only updates switches in the VTP client mode that have a higher VTP revision number.

F. A switch in the VTP server mode will update switches in the VTP client mode regardless of the configured VTP domain membership.

Answer: ABD

**199. Refer to the exhibit. Both switches are using a default configuration. Which two destination addresses will host 4 use to send data to host 1? (Choose two.)**

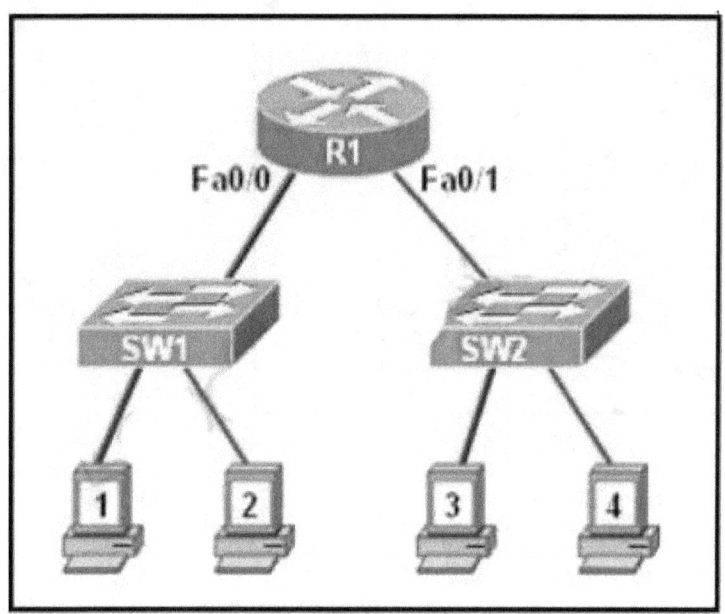

A. the IP address of host 1
B. the IP address of host 4
C. the MAC address of host 1
D. the MAC address of host 4
E. the MAC address of the Fa0/0 interface of the R1 router
F. the MAC address of the Fa0/1 interface of the R1 router

Answer: AF

**200. What are two reasons a network administrator would use CDP? (Choose two.)**

A. to verify the type of cable interconnecting two devices
B. to determine the status of network services on a remote device
C. to obtain VLAN information from directly connected switches
D. to verify Layer 2 connectivity between two devices when Layer 3 fails
E. to obtain the IP address of a connected device in order to telnet to the device
F. to determine the status of the routing protocols between directly connected routers

Answer: DE

**201. Refer to the exhibit. The router has been configured with these commands:**

```
hostname Gateway
interface FastEthernet 0/0
 ip address 198.133.219.14 255.255.255.248
 no shutdown
interface FastEthernet 0/1
 ip address 192.168.10.254 255.255.255.0
 no shutdown
interface Serial 0/0
 ip address 64.100.0.2 255.255.255.252
 no shutdown
ip route 0.0.0.0 0.0.0.0 64.100.0.1
```

What are the two results of this configuration? (Choose two.)

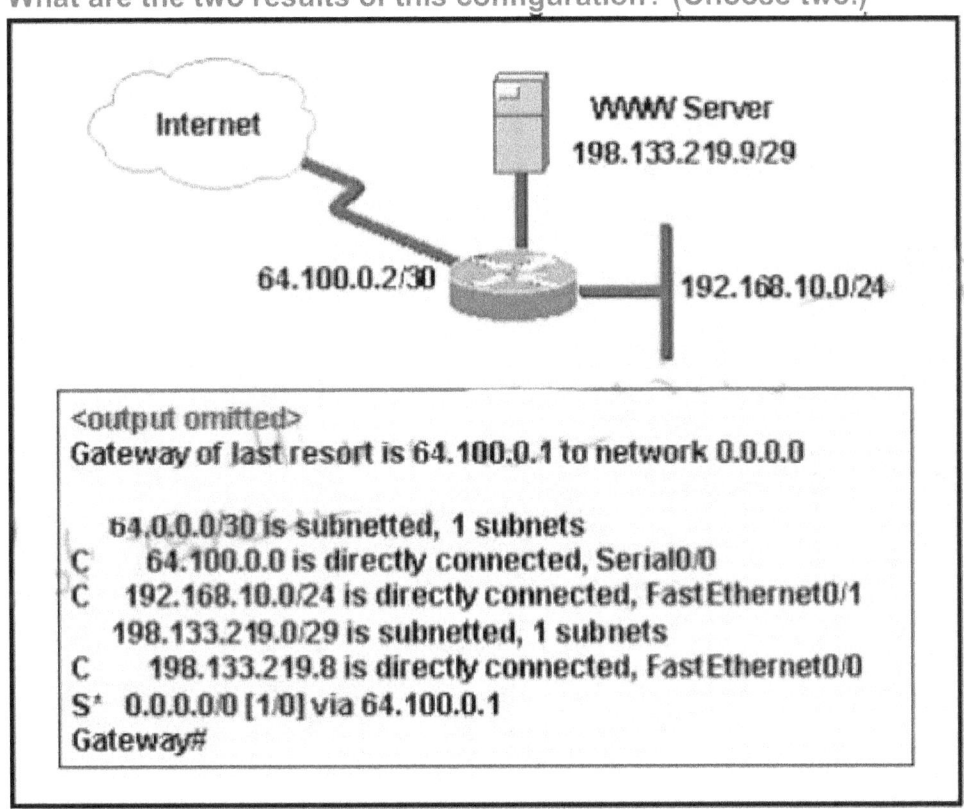

A. The default route should have a next hop address of 64.100.0.3.
B. Hosts on the LAN that is connected to FastEthernet 0/1 are using public IP addressing.
C. The address of the subnet segment with the WWW server will support seven more servers.
D. The addressing scheme allows users on the Internet to access the WWW server.
E. Hosts on the LAN that is connected to FastEthernet 0/1 will not be able to access the Internet without address translation.

Answer: DE

202. A company is installing IP phones. The phones and office computers connect to the same device. To ensure maximum throughput for the phone data, the company needs to make sure that the phone traffic is on a different network from that of the office computer data traffic. What is the best network device to which to directly connect the phones and computers, and what technology should be implemented on this device? (Choose two.)

A. hub
B. router
C. switch
D. STP
E. subinterfaces
F. VLAN

Answer: CF

203. What are two benefits of using VTP in a switching environment? (Choose two.)

A. It allows switches to read frame tags.
B. It allows ports to be assigned to VLANs automatically.
C. It maintains VLAN consistency across a switched network.
D. It allows frames from multiple VLANs to use a single interface.
E. It allows VLAN information to be automatically propagated throughout the switching environment.

Answer: CE

204. Which two statements are true about the command ip route 172.16.3.0 255.255.255.0 192.168.2.4? (Choose two.)

A. It establishes a static route to the 172.16.3.0 network.
B. It establishes a static route to the 192.168.2.0 network.
C. It configures the router to send any traffic for an unknown destination to the 172.16.3.0 network.
D. It configures the router to send any traffic for an unknown destination out the interface with the
address 192.168.2.4.
E. It uses the default administrative distance.
F. It is a route that would be used last if other routes to the same destination exist.

Answer: AE

205. What are two advantages of Layer 2 Ethernet switches over hubs? (Choose two.)

A. decreasing the number of collision domains
B. filtering frames based on MAC addresses
C. allowing simultaneous frame transmissions

D. increasing the size of broadcast domains
E. increasing the maximum length of UTP cabling between devices

Answer: BC

206. Refer to the exhibit. A network associate needs to configure the switches and router in the graphic so that the hosts in VLAN3 and VLAN4 can communicate with the enterprise server in VLAN2. Which two Ethernet segments would need to be configured as trunk links? (Choose two.)

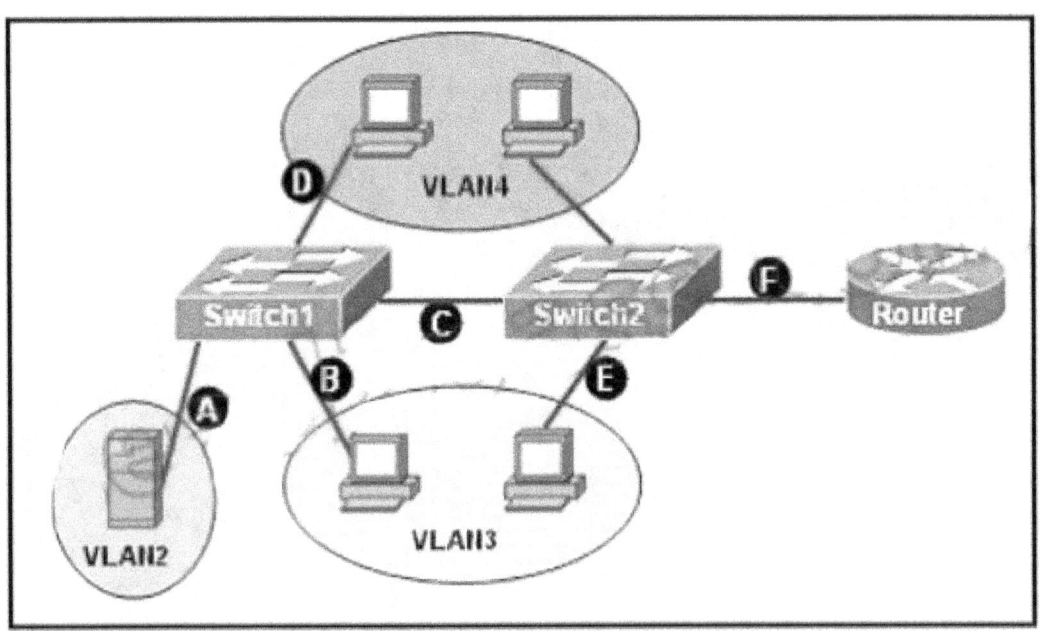

A. A
B. B
C. C
D. D
E. E
F. F

Answer: CF

207. Which two values are used by Spanning Tree Protocol to elect a root bridge? (Choose two.)

A. amount of RAM
B. bridge priority
C. IOS version
D. IP address
E. MAC address
F. speed of the links

Answer: BE

208. Refer to the exhibit. The networks connected to router R2 have been summarized as a 192.168.176.0/21 route and sent to R1. Which two packet destination addresses will R1 forward to R2? (Choose two.)

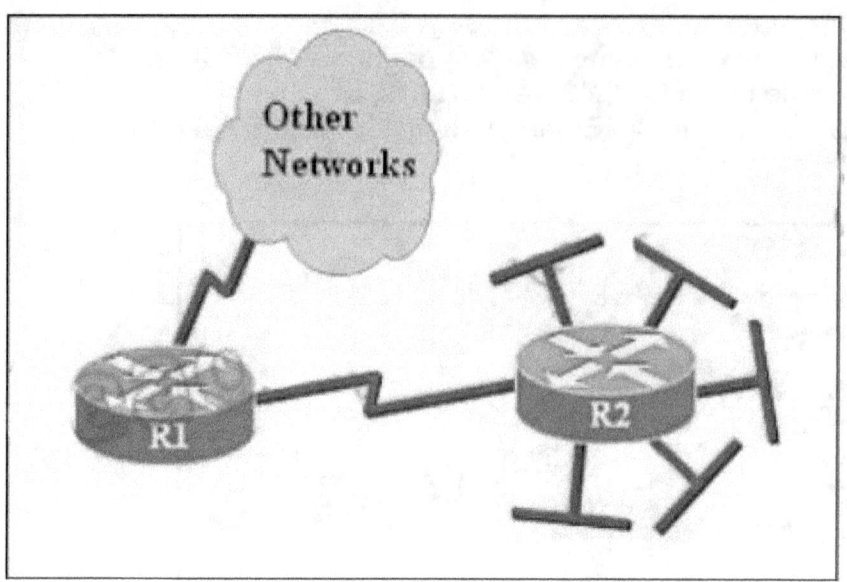

A. 192.168.194.160
B. 192.168.183.41
C. 192.168.159.2
D. 192.168.183.255
E. 192.168.179.4
F. 192.168.184.45

Answer: BE

209. Which three statements are typical characteristics of VLAN arrangements? (Choose three.)

A. A new switch has no VLANs configured.
B. Connectivity between VLANs requires a Layer 3 device.
C. VLANs typically decrease the number of collision domains.
D. Each VLAN uses a separate address space.
E. A switch maintains a separate bridging table for each VLAN.
F. VLANs cannot span multiple switches.

Answer: BDE

210. Refer to the exhibit. Which three statements are true about how router JAX will choose a path to the 10.1.3.0/24 network when different routing protocols are configured? (Choose three.)

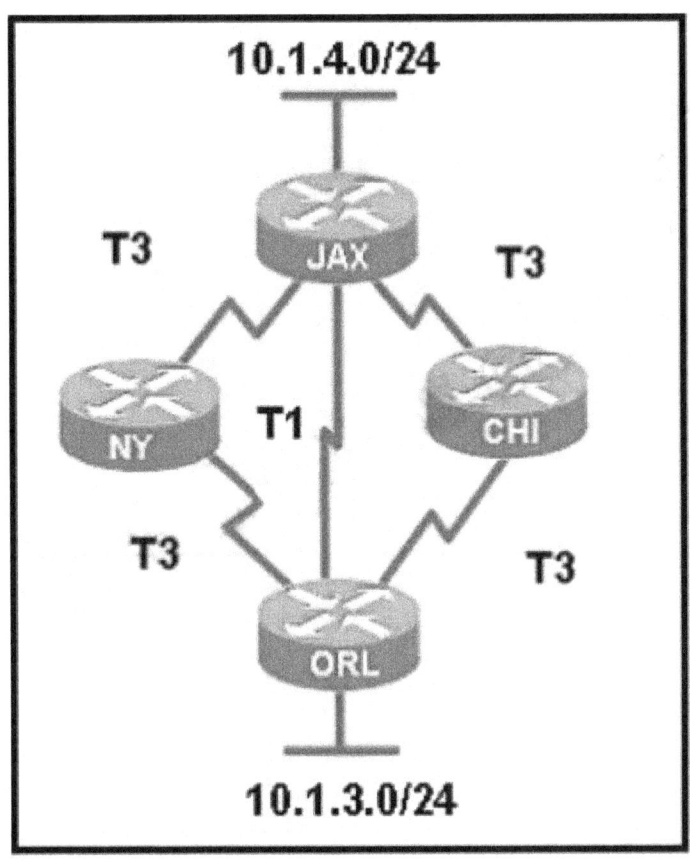

A. By default, if RIPv2 is the routing protocol, only the path JAX-ORL will be installed into the routing table.
B. The equal cost paths JAX-CHI-ORL and JAX- NY-ORL will be installed in the routing table if RIPv2
is the routing protocol.
C. When EIGRP is the routing protocol, only the path JAX-ORL will be installed in the routing table by default.
D. When EIGRP is the routing protocol, the equal cost paths JAX-CHI-ORL, and JAX-NY-ORL will be
installed in the routing table by default.
E. With EIGRP and OSPF both running on the network with their default configurations, the EIGRP paths
will be installed in the routing table.
F. The OSPF paths will be installed in the routing table, if EIGRP and OSPF are both running on the
network with their default configurations.

Answer: ADE

211. Refer to the exhibit. Which three statements correctly describe Network Device A? (Choose three.)

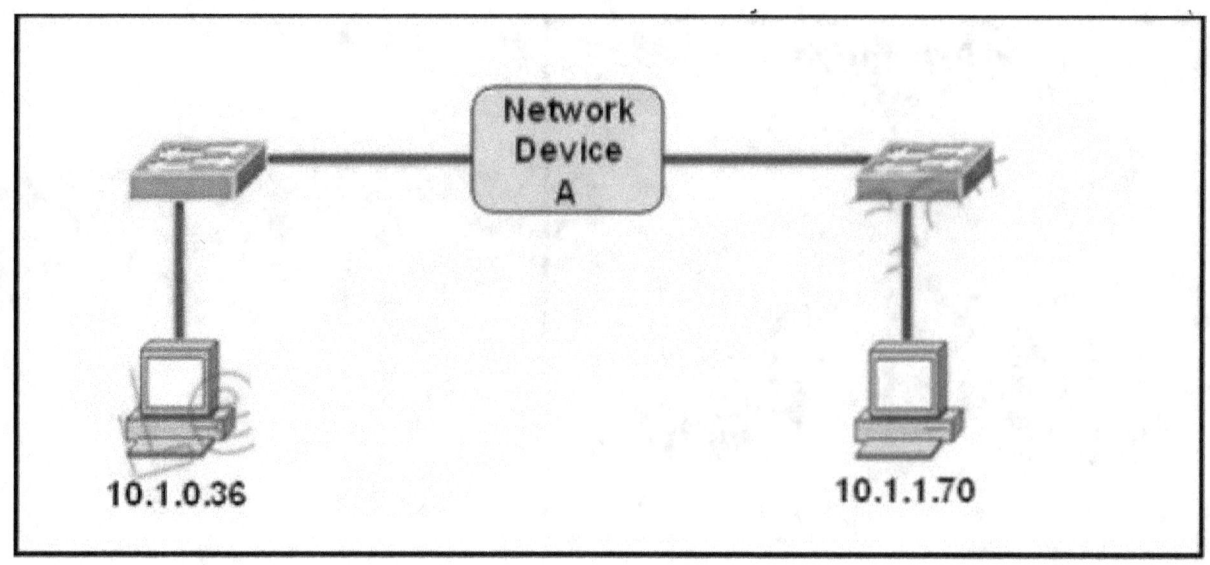

A. With a network wide mask of 255.255.255.128, each interface does not require an IP address.
B. With a network wide mask of 255.255.255.128, each interface does require an IP address on a
unique IP subnet.
C. With a network wide mask of 255.255.255.0, must be a Layer 2 device for the PCs to communicate
with each other.
D. With a network wide mask of 255.255.255.0, must be a Layer 3 device for the PCs to communicate
with each other.
E. With a network wide mask of 255.255.254.0, each interface does not require an IP address.

Answer: BDE

212. Switch ports operating in which two roles will forward traffic according to the IEEE 802.1w standard? (Choose two.)

A. alternate
B. backup
C. designated
D. disabled
E. root

Answer: CE

213. Refer to the exhibit. Given the output shown from this Cisco Catalyst 2950, what is the most likely reason that interface FastEthernet 0/10 is not the root port for VLAN 2?

```
Switch# show spanning-tree interface fastethernet0/10
Vlan              Role Sts Cost       Prio.Nbr Type
----------------- ---- --- ---------- -------- ----
VLAN0001          Root FWD 19          128.1    P2p
VLAN0002          Altn BLK 19          128.2    P2p
VLAN0003          Root FWD 19          128.2    P2p
```

A. This switch has more than one interface connected to the root network segment in VLAN 2.
B. This switch is running RSTP while the elected designated switch is running 802.1d Spanning Tree.
C. This switch interface has a higher path cost to the root bridge than another in the topology.
D. This switch has a lower bridge ID for VLAN 2 than the elected designated switch.

Answer: C

214. Refer to the exhibit. This command is executed on 2960Switch:
2960Switch(config)# mac-address-table static 0000.00aa.aaaa vlan 10 interface fa0/1
Which two of these statements correctly identify results of executing the command? (Choose two.)

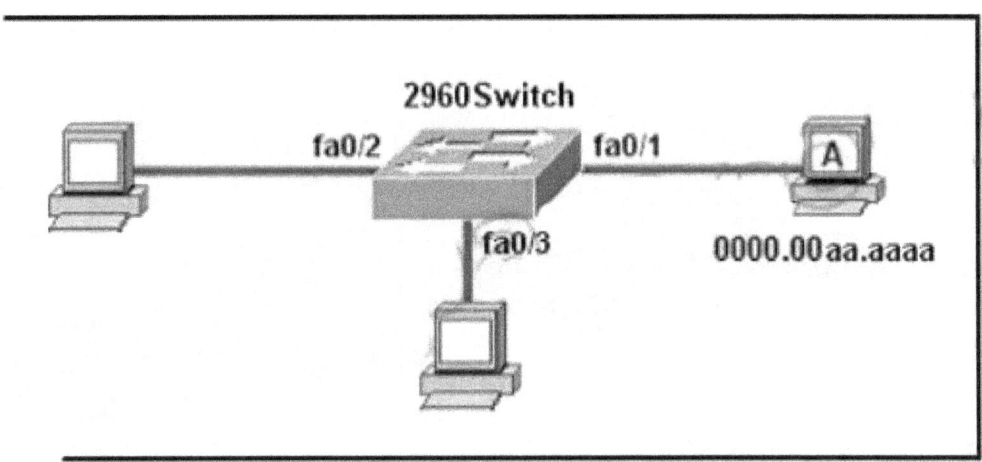

A. Port security is implemented on the fa0/1 interface.
B. MAC address 0000.00aa.aaaa does not need to be learned by this switch.
C. Only MAC address 0000.00aa.aaaa can source frames on the fa0/1 segment.
D. Frames with a Layer 2 source address of 0000.00aa.aaaa will be forwarded out fa0/1.
E. MAC address 0000.00aa.aaaa will be listed in the MAC address table for interface fa0/1 only.

Answer: BE

215. Which of the following describes the roles of devices in a WAN? (Choose three.)

A. A CSU/DSU terminates a digital local loop.
B. A modem terminates a digital local loop.

C. A CSU/DSU terminates an analog local loop.
D. A modem terminates an analog local loop.
E. A router is commonly considered a DTE device.
F. A router is commonly considered a DCE device.

Answer: ADE

**216. What are two characteristics of Telnet? (Choose two.)**

A. It sends data in clear text format.
B. It is no longer supported on Cisco network devices.
C. It is more secure than SSH.
D. It requires an enterprise license in order to be implemented.
E. It requires that the destination device be configured to support Telnet connections.

Answer: AE

**217. What are two security appliances that can be installed in a network? (Choose two.)**

A. ATM
B. IDS
C. IOS
D. IOX
E. IPS
F. SDM

Answer: BE

**218. Assuming a subnet mask of 255.255.248.0, three of the following addresses are valid host addresses. Which are these addresses? (Choose three.)**

A. 172.16.9.0
B. 172.16.8.0
C. 172.16.31.0
D. 172.16.20.0

Answer: ACD

www.ingramcontent.com/pod-product-compliance
Lightning Source LLC
Chambersburg PA
CBHW060416220526
45465CB00008B/2903